Microwave Magic
Oriental Cooking

Grolier Limited
TORONTO

Contributors to this series:

Recipes and Technical Assistance:
École de cuisine Bachand-Bissonnette
Cooking consultants:
Denis Bissonette
Michèle Émond
Dietician:
Christiane Barbeau
Photos:
Laramée Morel Communications
Audio-Visuelles
Design:
Claudette Taillefer
Assistants:
Julie Deslauriers
Philippe O'Connor
Joan Pothier
Accessories:
Andrée Cournoyer
Writing:
Communications La Griffe Inc.
Text Consultants:
Cap et bc inc.
Advisors:
Roger Aubin
Joseph R. De Varennes
Gaston Lavoie
Kenneth H. Pearson

Assembly:
Carole Garon
Vital Lapalme
Jean-Pierre Larose
Carl Simmons
Gus Soriano
Marc Vallières
Production Managers:
Gilles Chamberland
Ernest Homewood
Production Assistants:
Martine Gingras
Catherine Gordon
Kathy Kishimoto
Peter Thomlison
Art Director:
Bernard Lamy
Editors:
Laurielle Ilacqua
Susan Marshall
Margaret Oliver
Robin Rivers
Lois Rock
Jocelyn Smyth
Donna Thomson
Dolores Williams
Development:
Le Groupe Polygone Éditeurs Inc.

We wish to thank the following firms, PIER I IMPORTS and LE CACHE POT, for their contribution to the illustration of this set.

The series editors have taken every care to ensure that the information given is accurate. However, no cookbook can guarantee the user successful results. The editors cannot accept any responsibility for the results obtained by following the recipes and recommendations given.

Canadian Cataloguing in Publication Data

Main entry under title:

Oriental cooking

(Microwave magic ; 18)
Translation of: La Cuisine orientale.
Includes index.
ISBN 0-7172-2439-2

1. Microwave cookery (Game).   2. Cookery, Oriental.
I. Series: Microwave magic (Toronto, Ont.) ; 18.

TX832.C8513 1988   641.5'882   C88-094217-7

Contents

Microwave Magic is a multi-volume set, with each volume devoted to a particular type of cooking. So, if you are looking for a chicken recipe, you simply go to one of the two volumes that deal with poultry. Each volume has its own index, and the final volume contains a general index to the complete set.

Microwave Magic puts over twelve hundred recipes at your fingertips. You will find it as useful as the microwave oven itself. Enjoy!

Note from the Editor

How to Use this Book
The books in this set have been designed to make your job as easy as possible. As a result, most of the recipes are set out in a standard way.

We suggest that you begin by consulting the information chart for the recipe you have chosen. You will find there all the information you need to decide if you are able to make it: preparation time, cost per serving, level of difficulty, number of calories per serving and other relevant details. Thus, if you have only 30 minutes in which to prepare the evening meal, you will quickly be able to tell which recipe is possible and suits your schedule.

The list of ingredients is always clearly separated from the main text. When space allows, the ingredients are shown together in a photograph so that you can make sure you have them all without rereading the list—

another way of saving your valuable time. In addition, for the more complex recipes we have supplied photographs of the key stages involved either in preparation or serving.

All the dishes in this book have been cooked in a 700 watt microwave oven. If your oven has a different wattage, consult the conversion chart that appears on the following page for cooking times in different types of oven. We would like to emphasize that the cooking times given in the book are a minimum. If a dish does not seem to be cooked enough, you may return it to the oven for a few more minutes. Also, the cooking time can vary according to your ingredients: their water and fat content, thickness, shape and even where they come from. We have therefore left a blank space on each recipe page in which you can note

the cooking time that suits you best. This will enable you to add a personal touch to the recipes that we suggest and to reproduce your best results every time.

Although we have put all the technical information together at the front of this book, we have inserted a number of boxed entries called **MICROTIPS** throughout to explain particular techniques. They are brief and simple, and will help you obtain successful results in your cooking.

With the very first recipe you try, you will discover just how simple microwave cooking can be and how often it depends on techniques you already use for cooking with a conventional oven. If cooking is a pleasure for you, as it is for us, it will be all the more so with a microwave oven. Now let's get on with the food.

The Editor

Key to the Symbols
For ease of reference, the following symbols have been used on the recipe information charts.

The pencil symbol ✏ is a reminder to write your cooking time in the space provided.

Level of Difficulty

🍴 Easy

🍴🍴 Moderate

🍴🍴🍴 Complex

Cost per Serving

$ Inexpensive

$ $ Moderate

$ $ $ Expensive

Power Levels

All the recipes in this book have been tested in a 700 watt oven. As there are many microwave ovens on the market with different power levels, and as the names of these levels vary from one manufacturer to another, we have decided to give power levels as a percentage. To adapt the power levels given here, consult the chart opposite and the instruction manual for your oven.

Generally speaking, if you have a 500 watt or 600 watt oven you should increase cooking times by about 30% over those given, depending on the actual length of time required. The shorter the original cooking time, the greater the percentage by which it must be lengthened. The 30% figure is only an average. Consult the chart for detailed information on this topic.

Power Levels

HIGH: 100% - 90%	Vegetables (except boiled potatoes and carrots) Soup Sauce Fruits Browning ground beef Browning dish Popcorn
MEDIUM HIGH: 80% - 70%	Rapid defrosting of precooked dishes Muffins Some cakes Hot dogs
MEDIUM: 60% - 50%	Cooking tender meat Cakes Fish Seafood Eggs Reheating Boiled potatoes and carrots
MEDIUM LOW: 40%	Cooking less tender meat Simmering Melting chocolate
DEFROST: 30% **LOW: 30% - 20%**	Defrosting Simmering Cooking less tender meat
WARM: 10%	Keeping food warm Allowing yeast dough to rise

Cooking Time Conversion Chart

700 watts	600 watts*
5 s	11 s
15 s	20 s
30 s	40 s
45 s	1 min
1 min	1 min 20 s
2 min	2 min 40 s
3 min	4 min
4 min	5 min 20 s
5 min	6 min 40 s
6 min	8 min
7 min	9 min 20 s
8 min	10 min 40 s
9 min	12 min
10 min	13 min 30 s
20 min	26 min 40 s
30 min	40 min
40 min	53 min 40 s
50 min	66 min 40 s
1 h	1 h 20 min

* There is very little difference in cooking times between 500 watt ovens and 600 watt ovens.

The Splendors and Mysteries of China

In presenting this volume, *Oriental Cooking,* we feel an explanation of our choice of title is in order to avoid confusion among our readers. Oriental cooking in fact encompasses cuisine from a very large territory, of which China is only a part. Be that as it may, we have devoted this volume exclusively to culinary principles and dishes of China. We find justification for this in the fact that over the centuries Chinese cooking has had considerable influence on the other Asiatic countries, where it has been a very real source of culinary inspiration. Among the countries that have adopted the main principles of Chinese cooking as their own, we can name Thailand, Vietnam and Korea among others in that general area. However, it is not only neighboring countries that have profited from this enriching influence. The West, as well, has succumbed to the charms of Chinese cuisine—witness the number of Chinese restaurants and markets in North American cities.

We would also like to point out that *International Cuisine,* Volume 24, contains some information on Japanese cooking for interested readers. While the Western world may be enthusiastic about Chinese cooking, its basic principles are still something of a mystery to most of us. For this reason, we are going to take you on a short excursion into this world, where cooking is a fine art.

China consists of four major regions which, because of their respective culinary specialities, have each contributed to the diversity of this vast country's culinary repertoire.

Northern China, noted for its Peking duck, was for a long time considered the capital of the Chinese empire. Besides Peking, there are the provinces of Ho-Nan and Chang-Tong in the north. These northern provinces use wheat rather than rice in their cooking; the northern climate making rice growing impossible. Wheat is used to make the noodles, dumplings and little pancakes typical of their cuisine. This region is also noted for its sweet and sour sauces and the delicacy of its spices.

Further south we have the city of Shanghai, best known for its swallow's nest soup, and Fu-Kien, which is known for its "red cooking." This maritime province, with over 5000 kilometers of coastline, excels in the preparation of fish and seafood dishes. It is also well known for its delicious soups.

The interior region of the country offers the more highly spiced, richly flavored Szechuan cooking. This school of cooking, becoming more and more popular in our country, has developed its own distinctive style and is a favorite of gourmets.

Finally, we arrive at the southern regions of the country, where the most diversified and most well-known cooking was developed. Canton, the home of Cantonese cooking, has several specialities. The highly regarded delicacy, shark fin soup, is found in this region. We must also thank the Cantonese for their oyster sauce, an indispensable ingredient in Chinese cooking.

Regardless of the region of its origin, Chinese cooking has the advantage of combining good nutrition with superb flavor—the rapid method of cooking preserves all the nutrients in the food. For example, the stir-frying or steaming of vegetables preserves their vitamins and minerals. As well, the frequent use of seafood in Chinese recipes provides the protein necessary to a balanced diet. As well as being very economical, Chinese cooking offers a great deal of variety in the number of dishes to choose from.

Adaptability and creativity play important roles in this type of cooking, followed closely by a sense of harmony.

Some Basic Ingredients

Rice: China's Daily Staple

The one food that is indispensable to the Asiatic people is rice. In fact this food, essential to Chinese cooking, nourishes at least a third of the world's population. An irreplaceable staple in the diet of our neighbors on the other side of the world, rice is to them what bread is to us.

You may be surprised to learn that there are close to 7000 varieties of rice around the world, the shapes, colors and textures varying greatly from one kind to another. For example, there is long grain rice and short grain rice, rice varying in color from white to violet and from beige to red and different types containing different quantities of starch. In the West white rice is the most common and most other varieties are unknown.

For the sake of simplicity we shall consider only three categories of rice: short grain, medium grain and long grain—admittedly, a somewhat scanty summary. Short and medium grain rices contain more starch than long grain and do not always maintain a firm texture after cooking. These varieties are traditionally used in oriental cooking, but long grain rice is being used more frequently of late, perhaps because the grains remain quite firm and do not stick to each other when cooked.

It should not be concluded that varieties containing more starch are of no value; some

10

Asiatic people, such as the Japanese, use rice in a much different way than we do. They will serve a starchier rice with dishes that it complements very nicely.

While it is one of the world's largest consumers of rice, China is not the only country where rice is grown. Rice plantations can be found in Europe as well as in America. Different varieties are important exports for several countries of the world, as rice is appreciated internationally. In regions of the world where famine and disasters are a constant menace, it is important to be able to provide staples that are easily and quickly produced. Asiatic people continue to cultivate rice by traditional methods and do not use any machinery to speak of. Barefoot in the flooded rice paddies, bent over, the workers plant the young rice shoots in the wet earth. They also irrigate the paddies manually, emptying buckets one at a time into small feeder canals. These methods, ancient and outmoded as they may seem to Westerners, are still in use in several regions of China.

Rice, when combined with vegetables, fish and meat, provides all the essential elements of a balanced diet. This grain, which Confucius praised with such fervor, contains considerable amounts of minerals and starch. Rough, unpolished rice provides protein and Vitamin B. Polished rice, such as white rice, has lost much of its nutritional value. However, some Western producers compensate for this loss by processing polished rice in such a way that some of its nutrients are retained.

Rice accompanies most meals in most regions of China—its absence would be unthinkable. As bread holds a prominent place in our stories and legends, the tales of faraway China convey the customs of its people; rice, a symbol of fertility, is often sprinkled over newlyweds as they emerge from their wedding ceremony. But don't wait for a wedding before trying this nutritious and versatile food.

Other Grains and Cereals

Certain regions do not have a climate favorable to the cultivation of rice. Thus, in northern China, where we find Peking and Ho-Nan, wheat is substituted for rice in several dishes. As well as wheat, barley, millet and buckwheat are often used to accompany Chinese dishes.

Flour extracted from wheat is used in the making of noodles and dumplings of different sizes and shapes. They are usually served fried, as a garnish for soups or with a sauce. One of the great features of Oriental cooking lies in its artistic potential—why not make maximum use of the products available by creating great new dishes?

Meat

In China and its neighboring countries, pork, beef and, occasionally, lamb constitute the basis of many meals, as they do in this country. From East to West these meats enjoy great popularity among gourmets, but they vary greatly in their methods of preparation. By experimenting with the techniques outlined in this book, you will learn the many subtleties of Chinese cooking.

When it comes to red meat, pork is the first choice for the consumer in China, the tenderloin and spareribs being the most popular cuts. Beef takes second place on the list of meats most desirable for Chinese dishes; again, it is the tenderloin that is the choice cut. Lamb, rather fatty and having a strong flavor that overpowers other ingredients, is not widely used except in the north. The cuts usually in demand are the loin, the leg and the shoulder. While many of these meat cuts are expensive, it is important not to substitute cheaper ones as the entire dish will suffer for it.

In Chinese cooking, meat, whether served in slices, cut in strips or ground and formed into balls, must be tender and have a delicate flavor. In the preparation process, the cutting of the meat and the cooking are equally important, both requiring skill and patience. See page 102, "Preparing A ⟹

Chinese Meal," for a detailed explanation of the cutting and cooking techniques used in Chinese cooking.

Poultry

Chicken and duck are especially prized and their use results in some exceptionally delicious creations. While we may excel in preparing many different dishes with chicken, our versatility does not compare with the thousand and one ways in which it is prepared in the Asiatic countries. As certain regions are noted for their soups or for their unique seasonings, Peking is noted among gourmets the world over for its famous duck. Peking duck has an unforgettable flavor, even with the many outstanding tastes and smells that accompany a Chinese meal.

Note that in Chinese cooking, if poultry is to be served whole the flesh must pull away from the carcass easily. A well-done bird is a delight to eat.

Variety Meats

Several Chinese dishes also make use of organ, or variety, meats. For example, liver and kidneys from both meat and poultry are delicious with vegetable dishes. This type of meat, as well as the more traditional kinds of meat, is cut into fine pieces—an art which requires a bit of practice on your part.

To insist that Chinese methods are healthier than our cooking habits might seem exaggerated to some. However, whether steamed, sautéed or roasted, meat and poultry prepared the Chinese way retain all their flavor and are very lean. This is partly due to the fact that butter and animal fats are never used, as they are in the West; only vegetable oils such as peanut or soybean oil are used. You will find more on this subject in the section on cooking oils on page 19 of this volume.

The Oceans Hold a Thousand Treasures

Fish and Seafood

Do any of these names—Kiang shrimp, Tsao Ku scallops, Mi-Chiu trout—bring exotic images to mind? At the very least, one must admit that they would certainly arouse the curiosity of any gourmet ready to be seduced by Chinese cooking.

Perhaps you have come across someone of Asiatic origin at the fish market and wondered what kind of miniature monster resided in his basket. Maybe you even had the courage to ask what he had bought, where it came from and what he intended to do with it. But you, yourself, need not start your experiments in Chinese cooking with strange and exotic dishes. A few explanations, however, about the gastronomic habits of the Chinese consumer won't hurt the development of your taste for oriental cuisine.

The variety of fish and seafood used in Chinese dishes is unbelievable. This massive country boasts 5000 kilometers of coastline where the waves of the China Sea and the Yellow Sea provide quantities of seafood, each variety more colorful than the next. As well, numerous lakes assure a supply of freshwater fish to the inland villages.

Oysters, squid, shrimp, shark, bass and plaice are but a few of the species that find their way to a Chinese kitchen. All the regional schools of cooking attach great importance to fish and seafood of all kinds. Frequently, if they are to be consumed immediately, they are bought alive and kept in water right up to the time of preparation. Then again, they may also be dried, in which case they can be kept for a longer period of time; the drying process also makes for a much stronger flavor.

Differences in climate play an important part in the texture and flavor of foods; certain species, like crab and shrimp, will vary depending on where they are caught. Be that as it may, most of our fish and seafood can be adapted quite easily to oriental cuisine. Just as with other typically Chinese products, substitutes can usually be found to replace more exotic foods. Sometimes a recipe may call for a particular kind of fish that is not available in the West. In such cases, it is usually possible to obtain the item in question at speciality markets, either dried or in cans.

The methods of preparing these products of the sea vary according to the different regions, each one having its speciality. Steaming fish is by far the most popular cooking method among the Chinese, no doubt due to their preference for food that is light and fat-free. Also this method of cooking produces fish that is very tender and therefore easily removed from the bones with chopsticks.

Chinese chefs have developed a method of salting fish that not only preserves it but also gives it a flavor all its own, so unique that it has acquired an international reputation. Many oriental countries do a good job of cooking seafood, but it is the *savoir faire* of the Chinese that was the inspiration for our recipes for fish and seafood in this volume.

From the Gardens of China

Fruits and Vegetables

Chinese gardens are noted for variety in their produce, combining to create a fragrant mixture of scents and a harmonious blend of colors. "A garden on a plate!" you might say when offered an arrangement of oriental-style vegetables or fruit—a beautiful array of colors, textures and sometimes mysterious shapes. Such variety provides the subtle combination of flavors and textures characteristic of Chinese dishes, the produce of the land making them unique and thus adding to their appeal.

In spite of the extinction of the Ts'ing dynasty, which saw Chinese cuisine achieve glorious heights right up to the twentieth century, the Chinese people continue to cultivate the ancestral art of harmony in their cooking. The extraordinary variety of vegetables grown in China makes it possible to prepare interesting meals without meat or fish.

However, Chinese gourmets,

for whom a harmonious balance of elements is of prime importance, prefer to use all types of food in their cooking.

Some vegetables grow as easily in the West as they do in Asiatic countries, but there are some that remain indigenous to the Eastern countries. Fortunately, some of these vegetables are sold here in cans when they are not available fresh in speciality markets.

Fruit, used less frequently than vegetables, is not only used in desserts, for example, a delicious soup is concocted with winter melons. Also, the lotus root goes very well with vegetable dishes and plums are used to make a sauce for certain types of meat.

In fact, dessert does not play a prominent role in a Chinese meal. The "fortune cookies" found in Western shops and restaurants are not of Chinese origin. However, fruit is sometimes served at the end of a meal or as a refreshing snack. Of all Chinese fruit available in America, the best known is the lichee. Kumquats (small oranges that are sweet with an acidic flavor) and loquats (small yellow fruit, similar to plums) are available fresh and in cans. On the colorful shelves of the Chinese markets one finds, among other fruit, the lotus, to which some people ascribe magical properties. An aquatic plant, the lotus enjoys great popularity

because of its many uses. One can use the bulb from which the roots and the stalks grow; this bulb, when cut, produces lacy slices that are used decoratively as well as to impart a sweet flavor to dishes. The lotus roots are often used as a vegetable in recipes. The large green leaves that rise from the water and frame a lovely pink flower can be used to wrap various stuffings (rice, for example). Some dermatologists claim that the stamen from the lotus blossom has special properties to regenerate the skin.

However, the lotus is not the only exotic fruit to be found in oriental markets. There is also the famous water chestnut which some people especially enjoy with all the other ingredients in Chinese dishes. Slightly sweet and pleasant tasting, the water chestnut grows in stagnant waters.

When compiling a "Chinese" grocery list, one must not forget edible pea pods (which we know as snow peas), bamboo shoots and Chinese mushrooms. Leafy vegetables, such as Chinese parsley (with leaves larger than ours), Chinese cabbage and celery are readily obtainable in our supermarkets. No list would be complete without the addition of black beans, which highlight more than one Chinese dish.
Discovering all these strange, exotic foods remains one of

the great pleasures of this ancient form of cooking. Meanwhile, such vegetables as broccoli, asparagus and bean sprouts have been a mainstay of Chinese cooking as it has developed in this country.

Any helpful hints? Once the shopping is completed, allow yourself to enjoy the images these exotic foods evoke and let your imagination carry you back to ancient times when the emphasis was placed on the preparation of the meat. The individual steps for preparing a Chinese meal are explained in detail on pages 102 and 103 of this volume.

The Secrets of Chinese Cooking

Seasonings

All those intoxicating aromas that tickle your sense of smell as you wander down the narrow streets of Chinatown come from a world so different from ours that it seems impossible to reproduce them. And yet, the use of seasonings in Chinese cookery, while somewhat of an art, calls for relatively simple ingredients which can usually be found in local stores.

Whether used to enhance the natural flavor of foods or to alter their subtlety, certain spices are essential to Chinese cuisine. Each spice has its own special characteristic and often the spice is associated with certain dishes. For example, Szechuan pepper is an indispensable ingredient in Szechuan cookery. It gives the recipes a piquant taste that would be impossible to create with the peppers from India or Java, which are commonly used in our country.

Five spice powder, a mixture of anise, pepper, cloves, cinnamon and fennel, enhances game, poultry and fish to perfection. These foods are also complemented by the use of star anise, which has a surprising taste of licorice. Although these aromatics are among the most popular in China, one mustn't overlook the importance of ginger and coriander in Chinese cookery. These two flavoring agents, along with garlic, are always used fresh to obtain the maximum flavor. Curry, while of Indian origin, was quickly adopted by the Chinese. Because of its piquant taste this spice is very popular with Asiatic cooks.

Monosodium glutamate is another story, inspiring a lively controversy among Asiatic cooks. Prized by some because it enhances the taste of food, its use is strongly opposed by others who feel a chemical additive is unnecessary and prefer using natural seasonings. Also, it must be remembered that monosodium glutamate can cause severe allergic reactions in some individuals.

Dried Foods
There are other ways to create the magical aromas and flavors typical of Chinese cooking. One can use dried foods, adding them during the actual cooking. The Chinese are past masters at the art of mixing tastes while preserving the characteristics of each individual ingredient. The ability to season meat or fish dishes in this manner requires know-how and a good deal of experience.

However, there is nothing to prevent you from experimenting with the use of dried ingredients such as fragrant mushrooms, black mushrooms or the dried shrimp found in Chinese markets. Remember, such dried foods have a much stronger flavor and we recommend that smaller quantities be used.

Sauces
No discussion on seasoning would be complete without mention of the various sauces that determine the characteristic flavor of Chinese dishes. Among these, soy sauce is probably the most frequently used and is considered by some to be absolutely indispensable. This sauce is produced by allowing a mixture of wheat flour and soybean flour to ferment in salted water. It has a somewhat salty and tangy flavor; the milder, lighter form is served with soups, while the darker, more concentrated form is served with meat and fish dishes. Aside from soy sauce, oyster sauce, which is a speciality of the Cantonese school, is in frequent use, especially in that region. It enhances the flavor of meat and seafood without imposing a taste of its own. The delicious plum sauce must also be included among the favorites of the Chinese people. And let us not forget hoisin sauce, a delicious vegetable purée, sweet and spicy, which is sensational as a dip for seafood.

Cooking Oils
A final word must be said about the role of cooking oils in Chinese cooking. In fact, the flavor of the dishes to be prepared will depend greatly on the quality of oil used. For successful Chinese cooking it is important to use light oils, such as peanut oil or soybean oil, which impart a distinctive flavor to the food. One can also use sesame seed oil as a flavoring agent.

Substitutions: When Authentic Ingredients Are Unavailable

As any Chinese cook will tell you, one of the most important aspects of oriental culinary art is its capacity to adapt recipes to the resources of a region. The different schools of cookery have followed this principle since ancient times and have thus contributed to the diversity and the enrichment of the cuisine of China. Unfortunately, it is not always possible to obtain some of the ingredients called for in a recipe. It is quite permissible, therefore, to sustitute other equally delicious ingredients for items that are unavailable.

Authentic Ingredient	Substitute
Black beans	Soy sauce
Chinese cabbage	Swiss chard or spinach
Chinese dates (red)	Prunes
Kumquats	Oranges or tangerines
Lichees	Pears
Loquats	Peaches or apricots
Snow peas	Fresh or frozen green peas
Star anise	Extract of anise
Szechuan pepper	Crushed chili peppers
Wheat starch (thickener for sauces)	Cornstarch
Winter melon	Squash

Oriental Cooking in the Microwave: Utensils and Dishes

The invention of the microwave oven has revolutionized our cooking in many ways. Before its invention, who could have imagined cooking food in plastic containers in ovens with no heating elements? Plastic containers, in a surprising variety of sizes and shapes, are used routinely now.

Some of the dishes used in microwave cooking are more suitable for Chinese cooking than others. Glass bowls with covers and casserole dishes lend themselves very well to this type of cooking; if covers are lacking, plastic wrap will serve the purpose. There are, however, certain dishes especially designed for the microwave oven that are excellent for oriental cooking.

The browning dish can be substituted for the Chinese wok, as shown in the recipes throughout this volume. The bacon rack, with its grooved bottom, allows the cooking juices to drain away, preventing contact with the meat and therefore preventing it from cooking unevenly. There is another rack that, placed in a larger dish, serves the same purpose as the bacon rack. The browning dish and either rack can be substituted for the Chinese spit, used to roast large pieces of meat.

Food that should be steamed can be cooked in glass casseroles, preferably round to ensure uniform cooking. Microwaves cook food in corners more quickly than in the center of a dish. It is important to remember this fact, especially in Chinese cuisine, where the cooking makes all the difference. If you must use a square pan, shield the corners with strips of aluminum foil to prevent overcooking.

Oriental Cooking in the Microwave: Methods

One can easily adapt microwave cooking techniques to oriental cooking methods. In fact, the microwave oven offers many advantages, especially in that it allows a rapid and controlled method of cooking.

Steaming

Just like the Chinese experts you will, with the help of your microwave oven, be able to steam food, thereby letting it retain all its natural flavor. This is a technique that makes for lightness in cooking and is applicable to rice, meat, fish or vegetables. Steaming is a method used frequently in China; the cooking is effected by the action of the steam surrounding the food for varying lengths of time. In Asiatic countries, a large pot of boiling water is kept over a hot flame, thus producing quantities of steam that flow over food placed on grills above the pot. To ensure the best results with the microwave oven, it isn't necessary to use large amounts of water in order to steam food. The one exception to this is rice: two cups of liquid are necessary to cook one cup of rice. See the MICROTIPS on page 59 of this volume for more information on cooking rice.

What kind of dishes should be used to steam food in the microwave? It's up to you—choose traditional Chinese equipment where possible or use dishes especially developed for the microwave. The traditional bamboo steamer lends itself very well to microwave cooking. However, if you don't own one, you will manage just as well with a round or oval casserole or bowl with its own lid or covered with plastic wrap.

Very little liquid is necessary for steaming vegetables; 30 to 60 mL (2 to 4 tablespoons) is usually sufficient for 450 grams (1 lb) of vegetables. Vegetables are usually cut into small, thin strips and should not be cooked too long as they will lose their crisp texture as well as their nutrients.

As for meat, it can be poached in stock and fish, in a court bouillon.

Sautéing

Sautéing involves frying sliced food very lightly and quickly in a light oil, just long enough to impart a golden color. This cooking method is easily duplicated in the microwave oven with a browning dish, an indispensable dish for searing and roasting. Just as the Chinese do, you can sauté at high heat slices, cubes or strips of vegetables, fish or meat, always stirring often to ensure uniform cooking. This method can be used for several Chinese dishes; it will be to your advantage to learn the steps involved before attempting it.

Since the food is cut into small pieces, it does not normally require any more cooking after the searing process. Lightly cooked, the food will remain crisp and tender.

To sauté or to sear, you must heat the browning dish for 7 minutes at 100% before adding the required amount of oil or butter. In certain cases, the intense heat concentrated in the bottom of the dish is enough to sauté the food without returning it to the oven. If this proves to be the case, stir the contents several times with a wooden spoon. If the oil cools off too quickly, return it to the oven for a minute or two and then stir again.

This method of cooking is used mainly for food that is finely sliced and requires a brief cooking time.

Our eastern cousins also fry food in deep fat, a cooking method with which we are quite familiar. Certain foods are coated with batter or with eggs and crumbs and are fried in a large amount of oil. The microwave oven, however, is not conducive to deep fat frying.

Roasting

The "red cooking" mentioned earlier is concerned chiefly with the roasting of meat.

Traditionally cooked on a spit, the famous Chinese roast pork is tender and has a lovely golden color. Marinating the meat for several hours or, better still, several days, in a mixture of soy sauce, garlic and Chinese seasonings colors its surface, and imparts a delightful flavor to the meat and makes it very tender. Spit roasting is no doubt more suited to the oriental way of cooking than to ours. The pace of life and the utensils that are used in the Western world do not favor this kind of traditional cooking.

However, we can obtain results that are just as successful by using the microwave oven and the dishes at our disposal. As mentioned earlier, cuts that are to be roasted must be cooked raised on a rack so that they do not sit in their juices. Contact with the juices will cause those parts of the meat to cook more rapidly because liquids attract the microwaves. It is therefore advisable to use a rack with a grooved surface; a bacon rack or rack placed in a larger dish will certainly do the trick. It is also recommended that you sear, or brown, a roast before cooking it in your microwave oven. For more information on how to use the browning dish, turn to page 104 of this volume.

Honey-Glazed Chicken

Level of Difficulty	🍴
Preparation Time	20 min
Cost per Serving	$
Number of Servings	6
Nutritional Value	262 calories 35 g protein 254 mg sodium
Food Exchanges	3.5 oz meat
Cooking Time	53 min
Standing Time	10 min
Power Level	100%, 70%
Write Your Cooking Time Here	

Ingredients
1 1.8 kg (4 lb) chicken
3 leeks
15 mL (1 tablespoon) butter
15 mL (1 tablespoon) curry powder
30 mL (2 tablespoons) soy sauce
45 mL (3 tablespoons) honey
125 mL (1/2 cup) water
50 mL (1/4 cup) white wine
5 mL (1 teaspoon) Dijon mustard
15 mL (1 tablespoon) cornstarch dissolved in 45 mL (3 tablespoons) cold water

Method
— Slice the leeks into fine rings.
— Place the leeks in a dish; add the butter and curry powder.
— Cover and cook for 5 to 6 minutes at 100%; stir midway through the cooking.
— Pour the soy sauce into the cavity of the chicken and add the cooked leeks.
— Truss the chicken and brush with half the honey.
— Place the chicken on a rack in a dish, breast down.
— Pour the water and white wine into the dish with the chicken.
— Cook for 20 minutes at 70%, giving the dish a half-turn after 10 minutes of cooking.
— Turn the chicken over, breast up, and brush with the remaining honey.
— Continue to cook at 70% for 20 to 25 minutes or until the chicken is done, giving the dish a half-turn after 10 minutes of cooking.
— Remove the chicken from the oven, allow it to stand for 10 minutes, then keep it warm.
— To prepare the sauce, remove the rack and strain the collected juices.
— Add the Dijon mustard and dissolved cornstarch to the cooking juices and mix well.
— Cook the sauce for 1 to 2 minutes at 100%; stir halfway through the cooking time and again at the end.
— Carve the chicken and serve with the leeks and sauce.

Pork Tsung

Level of Difficulty	🍴
Preparation Time	20 min
Cost per Serving	$ $
Number of Servings	6
Nutritional Value	409 calories 35.2 g protein 8 mg iron
Food Exchanges	4 oz meat 1-1/2 vegetable exchanges 1-1/2 fat exchanges
Cooking Time	8 min
Standing Time	5 min
Power Level	100%
Write Your Cooking Time Here	🍎

Ingredients
900 g (2 lb) pork tenderloin, cut into strips
50 mL (1/4 cup) chicken broth
30 mL (2 tablespoons) cornstarch
30 mL (2 tablespoons) soy sauce
50 mL (1/4 cup) olive oil
250 mL (1 cup) bamboo shoots, cut into julienne strips
250 mL (1 cup) mushrooms, sliced
450 g (1 lb) bean sprouts
250 mL (1 cup) Chinese lettuce, sliced
50 mL (1/4 cup) green onion, sliced
10 mL (2 teaspoons) monosodium glutamate

Method
— Preheat a browning dish for 7 minutes at 100%.
— Meanwhile, mix the chicken broth, cornstarch and soy sauce and set aside.
— Pour the olive oil into the browning dish and heat for 30 seconds at 100%.
— Sear the strips of pork and pour the chicken broth mixture into the dish.
— Cover and cook at 100% for 2 to 4 minutes, stirring once during the cooking time.
— Add all the vegetables except the green onions; cover and cook for 3 to 4 minutes at 100%.
— Add the green onions and monosodium glutamate to the mixture; cover and let stand for 5 minutes before serving.

MICROTIPS

To Shell Shrimp

While it is always possible to use canned shrimps, many cooks prefer to use fresh ones. Shelling fresh shrimps is a simple matter. To make it even easier, purchase fairly large ones. Work your thumb under the shell along the length of the bottom of the shrimp, from head to tail, loosening it as you go. Then, using your thumbnail, cut the end of the shell where it is still attached at the joint between the body and the tail and peel the shell off the shrimp. The flesh of the shrimp should remain in one piece.

Chicken with Peanuts

Level of Difficulty	⦙⦙⦙
Preparation Time	30 min
Cost per Serving	S S
Number of Servings	6
Nutritional Value	424 calories 40.2 g protein 2.5 mg iron
Food Exchanges	4 oz meat 2 vegetable exchanges 2 fat exchanges
Cooking Time	6 min
Standing Time	5 min
Power Level	100%
Write Your Cooking Time Here	

Ingredients

900 g (2 lb) white meat of chicken, cut into strips
45 mL (3 tablespoons) oyster sauce
5 mL (1 teaspoon) monosodium glutamate
2 mL (1/2 teaspoon) sugar
5 mL (1 teaspoon) salt
125 mL (1/2 cup) oil
2 red peppers, cut into strips
2 green peppers, cut into strips
4 stalks of celery, cut into strips
2 onions, sliced
250 mL (1 cup) bamboo shoots, sliced
4 cloves garlic, finely chopped
50 mL (1/4 cup) green onions, sliced
125 mL (1/2 cup) peanuts

Method

— Preheat a browning dish for 7 minutes at 100%.
— In the meantime, mix the oyster sauce, monosodium glutamate, sugar and salt; set aside.
— Pour 50 mL (1/4 cup) of the oil into the dish and heat for 30 seconds at 100%.
— Sear the strips of chicken, remove from the oil and drain on a paper towel; set aside.
— Clean the browning dish; reheat for 7 minutes at 100%.
— Pour the remaining oil into the dish and heat for 30 seconds at 100%.
— Sear the peppers, celery, onions, bamboo shoots and garlic.
— Add the chicken and the oyster sauce mixture to the vegetables.
— Cover the dish and cook the entire mixture at 100% for 4 to 6 minutes, stirring once during the cooking time.

— Add the green onions and peanuts.
— Cover the dish and let it stand for 5 minutes before serving.

Once you've gathered all the ingredients, this delicious recipe can be prepared in short order, with excellent results.

Add the seared strips of chicken and the oyster sauce mixture to the vegetables after they have been seared in a browning dish.

Chicken with Broccoli

Level of Difficulty	🍴🍴
Preparation Time	30 min
Cost per Serving	**$**
Number of Servings	6
Nutritional Value	233 calories 38.4 g protein 2.3 mg iron
Food Exchanges	4 oz meat 1 vegetable exchange
Cooking Time	50 min
Standing Time	None
Power Level	70%, 100%, 90%
Write Your Cooking Time Here	

Ingredients
1 1.8 kg (4 lb) chicken
1 green onion, sliced
4 thin slices ginger root
250 mL (1 cup) chicken broth
3 thin slices Bayonne ham
1 bunch broccoli
10 mL (2 teaspoons) cornstarch dissolved in 15 mL (1 tablespoon) cold water

Method
— Place the chicken, breast down, in a casserole with the green onion and ginger. Pour the chicken broth over the chicken, basting it well.
— Cover the casserole and cook for 20 minutes at 70%.
— Turn the chicken over.
— Cover and continue cooking at 70% for 20 to 25 minutes or until the chicken is cooked.
— In the meantime, cut the ham into fairly wide strips, cut the broccoli into flowerets and slice the stalks into strips; set these ingredients aside.
— Remove the chicken from the casserole and remove the wings and legs. Set the legs and wings aside. Reserve the cooking juices.
— Cut the breast in two lengthwise and remove the meat from the breastbone. Cut the meat into 5 cm (2 in) pieces.
— Alternate the chicken pieces with the ham strips in a dish; place the legs and wings along the sides; cover and set aside.
— Place the broccoli in another dish and add 50 mL (1/4 cup) of the cooking juices.

— Cover and cook at 100% for 3 to 5 minutes or just enough to keep it crisp.
— Remove the broccoli and place it around the meat.
— Strain the remaining cooking juices and add the dissolved cornstarch; cook at 100% for 4 to 6 minutes, stirring twice during the cooking time.
— Pour the sauce over the meat.
— Cover and heat through for 3 to 4 minutes at 90%.
— Serve immediately.

Gather these few ingredients to prepare chicken with broccoli, an easy recipe that will impress your guests.

After removing the wings and legs of the cooked chicken, cut the breast meat into 5 cm (2 in) pieces.

Chicken with Pineapple

Ingredients

1.1 kg (2-1/2 lb) chicken breasts
1 whole pineapple
1 red pepper
1 green pepper
125 mL (1/2 cup) pineapple juice
125 mL (1/2 cup) orange juice
125 mL (1/2 cup) tomato juice
125 mL (1/2 cup) sugar
30 mL (2 tablespoons) cornstarch
50 mL (1/4 cup) vinegar
50 mL (1/4 cup) oil
1 540 mL (19 oz) can lichees

Method

— Slice the pineapple in two lengthwise.
— Cut the pineapple pulp from the shells and refrigerate the shells.
— Cut the pineapple pulp into cubes and set aside.
— Remove the chicken meat from the bones and cut into large cubes; set aside.
— Cut the peppers into a large dice and set aside.
— Mix the juices and add the sugar; cook at 100% for 5 to 6 minutes, stirring several times to make sure the sugar is dissolved.
— Dissolve the cornstarch in the vinegar and add to the hot juice mixture.
— Cook for 1 to 2 minutes at 100%; stirring once during the cooking time.
— Cover the sauce and set aside.
— Preheat a browning dish for 7 minutes at 100%; add the oil and heat for 30 seconds at 100%.
— Sear the chicken pieces, remove and set aside.
— Reheat the browning dish for 3 minutes at 100%.
— Sear the vegetables and pineapple cubes, then add the chicken and the warm sauce.
— Reduce the power to 90%, cover and cook for 7 to 9 minutes or until the chicken is cooked.
— Drain the lichees and add them to the mixture.
— Cover and allow the entire mixture to stand for 5 minutes.
— Pour the mixture into the pineapple shells and serve.

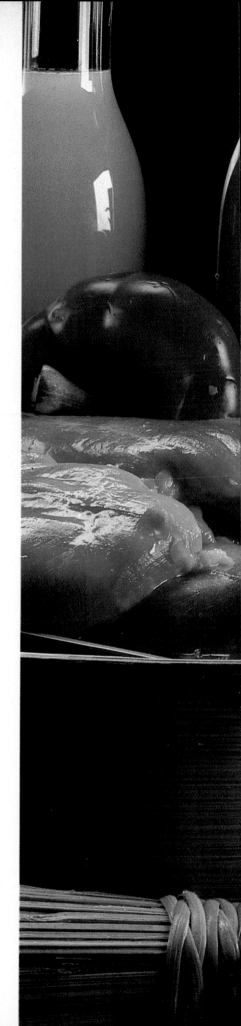

Duck in Aspic

Level of Difficulty	🍴🍴
Preparation Time	20 min*
Cost per Serving	$ $
Number of Servings	6
Nutritional Value	290 calories 36.8 g protein 2.6 mg iron
Food Exchanges	4 oz meat
Cooking Time	40 seconds
Standing Time	None
Power Level	100%
Write Your Cooking Time Here	

* This dish should be refrigerated for 3 hours before serving.

Ingredients
1 1.3 (3 lb) duck, roasted
225 g (8 oz) ham
1 envelope unflavored gelatin
50 mL (1/4 cup) cold water
3 chicken bouillon cubes
500 mL (2 cups) boiling water
5 mL (1 teaspoon) salt
2 mL (1/2 teaspoon) sake

Method
— Remove the meat from the bones of the duck.
— Cut the duck meat and the ham into fairly narrow slices.
— In a bowl, alternate layers of the duck and ham slices.
— Sprinkle the gelatin on the surface of the cold water and allow to soften for 2 minutes; stir once and heat for 30 to 40 seconds at 100%, making sure it does not boil.
— Dissolve the chicken cubes in the boiling water and add the gelatin, salt and sake; mix very well.
— Pour this mixture over the duck and ham slices.
— Refrigerate for 3 hours to allow the dish to set.

Assemble these ingredients before preparing this recipe for jellied duck, a tasty dish that your guests will enjoy.

Cut the duck meat and the ham into fairly narrow slices.

Before refrigerating, pour the chicken bouillon mixture over the slices of duck and cooked ham.

Chicken Lo Chou

Level of Difficulty	🍴🍴
Preparation Time	30 min
Cost per Serving	**S**
Number of Servings	8
Nutritional Value	229 calories 34.1 g protein 568 mg sodium
Food Exchanges	4 oz meat
Cooking Time	1 h 6 min
Standing Time	None
Power Level	100%, 70%
Write Your Cooking Time Here	

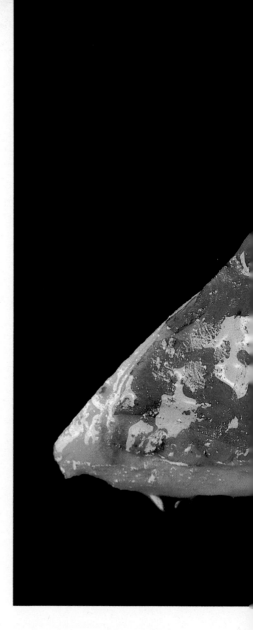

Ingredients
1 2.25 kg (5 lb) chicken
125 mL (1/2 cup) water
125 mL (1/2 cup) soy sauce
50 mL (1/4 cup) sake
5 thin slices ginger root
30 mL (2 tablespoons) sugar

Method
— Rinse the chicken and dry it carefully; set aside.
— In a casserole large enough to hold the chicken, mix all the ingredients except the sugar.
— Cook for 4 minutes at 100%.
— Place the chicken, breast up, in the casserole with the liquid and cover; reduce the power to 70% and cook for 30 minutes, basting the chicken twice with the liquid during the cooking time.
— Turn the chicken over, breast down, and add the sugar.
— Cover and continue cooking for 25 to 30 minutes at 70%, basting the chicken twice with its juices.
— Remove the wings and legs and cut the chicken in half lengthwise; remove the meat from the bones.
— Place each boneless breast flat, skin-side down, and cut the meat into rectangular pieces, 7 cm (3 in) by 2.5 cm (1 in).

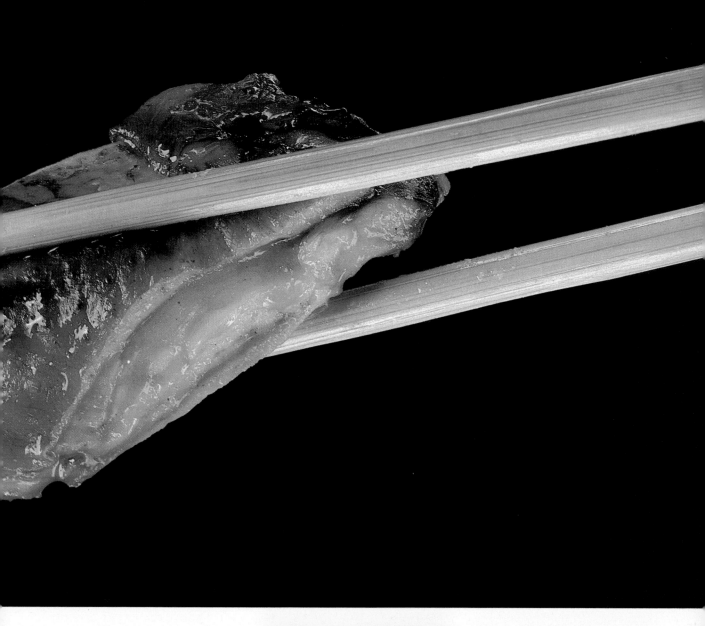

— Assemble the chicken pieces on a serving platter to look as much like a whole chicken breast as possible.
— Cut the wings and legs into similar pieces; add to the reconstructed chicken.
— Sprinkle the chicken with 50 mL (1/4 cup) of the cooking juices, and reheat at 100% for 1 to 2 minutes and serve immediately.

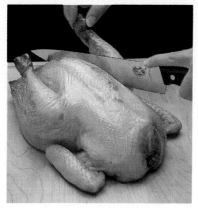

Remove the wings and legs before cutting the chicken in two lengthwise and then boning.

Cut the meat into rectangular pieces, 7 cm (3 in) by 2.5 cm (1 in).

Marinated Pork Tenderloin with Rice

Level of Difficulty	🍴
Preparation Time	15 min*
Cost per Serving	$ $
Number of Servings	3
Nutritional Value	657 calories 28 g protein 5.9 mg iron
Food Exchanges	3 oz meat 2 fruit exchanges 2 bread exchanges 3 fat exchanges
Cooking Time	12 min
Standing Time	None
Power Level	100%, 70%
Write Your Cooking Time Here	

MICROTIPS

To Cook Broccoli

It is not always easy to cook food that is irregular in shape. For example, broccoli stalks will cook more slowly than flowerets. You must therefore place the broccoli stalks toward the outside edge of the dish where the microwaves are more concentrated. Because they are placed in the center, the flowerets will not cook as quickly. Simple enough—when one knows the trick!

* The pork should be left to marinate for 1 hour before cooking.

Ingredients
340 g (12 oz) pork tenderloin
75 mL (1/3 cup) oil
750 mL (3 cups) cooked rice
15 mL (1 tablespoon) honey

Marinade:
10 mL (2 teaspoons) barbecue seasoning
10 mL (2 teaspoons) hoisin paste
5 mL (1 teaspoon) sesame paste
5 mL (1 teaspoon) sherry
6 green onions, sliced
125 mL (1/2 cup) sugar
75 mL (1/3 cup) soy sauce

Method
— Cut the tenderloin in half lengthwise and score it in several places with a knife.
— Place all the marinade ingredients in a bowl and mix well.
— Place the meat in the marinade for 1 hour.
— Remove the meat and set the marinade aside.
— Preheat a browning dish for 7 minutes at 100%; add the oil and heat for 30 seconds at 100%.
— Dry the meat well, sear and brush it with honey.
— Reduce the power to 70% and cook for 7 to 9 minutes, turning the meat over midway through the cooking time.
— Remove the meat and refrigerate.
— When the meat is cooled, cut it into thin slices.
— Divide the rice into 3 portions and place the slices of pork on top.
— Reheat the marinade for 1-1/2 to 2-1/2 minutes at 100%, stirring once.
— Pour the hot marinade over the meat and rice and serve.

Spareribs Chinese Style

Level of Difficulty	
Preparation Time	15 min
Cost per Serving	S
Number of Servings	2
Nutritional Value	517 calories 27.5 g protein 3.6 mg iron
Food Exchanges	3 oz meat 6 fat exchanges
Cooking Time	20 min
Standing Time	5 min
Power Level	100%, 70%
Write Your Cooking Time Here	

Ingredients
450 g (1 lb) pork spareribs, cut into 5 cm (2 in) pieces
15 mL (1 tablespoon) soy sauce
5 mL (1 teaspoon) sugar
15 mL (1 tablespoon) salted black beans, chopped
250 mL (1 cup) hot water
50 mL (1/4 cup) oil
2 cloves garlic, crushed
15 mL (1 tablespoon) cornstarch
50 mL (1/4 cup) cold beef broth

Method
— Preheat a browning dish for 7 minutes at 100%.
— In the meantime, mix the soy sauce, sugar, black beans and hot water to make a sauce and set aside.
— Add the oil to the browning dish and heat for 30 seconds at 100%.
— Sear the spareribs and garlic; cover the ribs with the sauce.
— Cover the dish and cook for 5 minutes at 100%.
— Stir, cover again and reduce the power to 70%; cook for 8 to 12 minutes or until the meat is tender and stir gently.
— Dissolve the cornstarch in the beef broth.
— Place the ribs on a serving dish, cover and set aside.
— With a spoon, skim the fat off the cooking juices.
— Pour the cornstarch and broth mixture into the browning dish and heat at 100% for 2 to 3 minutes, stirring twice during the cooking time.
— Cover the ribs with the sauce before serving.

This combination of ingredients results in a dish, the quality of which will be greatly appreciated by your guests.

Pour the sauce over the ribs after they have been seared in a browning dish.

Stir the ribs after their first cooking period and again at the end of their second period.

Lettuce Leaves Stuffed with Pork

Level of Difficulty	🍴🍴
Preparation Time	30 min*
Cost per Serving	S
Number of Servings	5
Nutritional Value	91.6 calories 13 g protein 330 mg sodium 3.2 mg iron
Food Exchanges	1 oz meat 1 vegetable exchange
Cooking Time	30 min
Standing Time	3 min
Power Level	100%
Write Your Cooking Time Here	

* Soak the Chinese mushrooms in hot water for 10 minutes before using.

Ingredients
20 leaves of Chinese lettuce
225 g (8 oz) pork, cut into strips
6 dried Chinese mushrooms
hot water
2 slices fresh ginger root, finely chopped
4 water chestnuts, finely chopped
2 green onions, sliced
15 mL (1 tablespoon) sake
15 mL (1 tablespoon) soy sauce
15 mL (1 tablespoon) oil
pepper to taste
575 mL (2-1/3 cups) water

Sauce:
30 mL (2 tablespoons) soy sauce
30 mL (2 tablespoons) sake
90 mL (6 tablespoons) chicken broth
2 green onions, sliced

Method
— Place the mushrooms in a bowl, cover with hot water and allow to soak for 10 minutes.
— Drain the mushrooms, remove the stems and discard.
— Dry the mushrooms caps very well and chop finely.

Lettuce Leaves Stuffed with Pork

Served as an hors d'oeuvre or as a main dish, this original recipe will really impress your guests. Here are the ingredients you will need.

Place the dried Chinese mushrooms in a bowl and cover with hot water; soak for 10 minutes.

After draining the mushrooms and removing the stems, chop the caps finely.

Place the lettuce leaves in a dish and pour boiling water over them. Cook for 3 minutes at 100% to blanch.

Place 15 mL (1 tablespoon) of the prepared stuffing on each lettuce leaf, roll the leaves up and secure with toothpicks.

Place the stuffed lettuce leaves on a rack in a dish and add 75 mL (1/3 cup) water to the bottom of dish; cover and cook for 13 to 15 minutes at 100%.

— Combine all the other ingredients except the lettuce leaves and water, add the chopped mushrooms, mix well and set the resulting stuffing aside.
— Bring 500 mL (2 cups) of the water to a boil by heating for 7 to 9 minutes at 100%.
— Place the lettuce leaves in a dish and cover with the boiling water.
— Cook for 3 minutes at 100% to blanch.
— Remove the lettuce leaves from the water and dry well.
— Place 15 mL (1 tablespoon) of the prepared stuffing on each lettuce leaf.
— Roll the lettuce leaves up and secure with toothpicks.
— Place the stuffed leaves on a rack in a dish.
— Pour the remaining 75 mL (1/3 cup) of water into the bottom of the dish; cover and cook at 100% for 13 to 15 minutes, giving the dish a half-turn midway through cooking time. Let stand for 3 minutes.
— Mix all the ingredients for the sauce and cook at 100% for 2 to 3 minutes, stirring once during the cooking time.
— Cover the stuffed lettuce leaves with the sauce just before serving.

Pork Kiang

Ingredients
450 g (1 lb) pork tenderloin
10 mL (2 teaspoons) cornstarch
30 mL (2 tablespoons) soy sauce
30 mL (2 tablespoons) oil
4 green onions, sliced
4 thin slices ginger root, cut into strips

Method
— Cut the pork tenderloin into strips.
— Dissolve the cornstarch in the soy sauce and oil to make a sauce.
— Place the pork in a dish, cover with the sauce and add the green onions and ginger.
— Cover and cook for 9 to 11 minutes at 70%; stirring twice during the cooking time.
— Let stand for 2 minutes before serving.

Level of Difficulty	🍴
Preparation Time	20 min
Cost per Serving	$ $
Number of Servings	4
Nutritional Value	294 calories 25.2 g protein 305 mg sodium
Food Exchanges	3 oz meat 1-1/2 fat exchanges
Cooking Time	11 min
Standing Time	2 min
Power Level	70%
Write Your Cooking Time Here	

Pork Meatballs

Level of Difficulty	🍴🍴
Preparation Time	30 min*
Cost per Serving	$ $
Number of Servings	4
Nutritional Value	294 calories 27.7 g protein 4.2 mg iron
Food Exchanges	3 oz meat 1 vegetable exchange 1/2 bread exchange
Cooking Time	9 min
Standing Time	2 min
Power Level	90%
Write Your Cooking Time Here	

* Soak the mushrooms for 30 minutes before preparing this recipe.

Ingredients
450 g (1 lb) lean ground pork
4 fragrant mushrooms
125 mL (1/2 cup) hot water
1 egg
15 mL (1 tablespoon) soy sauce
2 mL (1/2 teaspoon) salt
2 mL (1/2 teaspoon) sugar
5 mL (1 teaspoon) fresh ginger root, finely chopped
6 water chestnuts, finely chopped
1 green onion, finely chopped
250 mL (1 cup) rice, cooked
hot water

Method
— Put the mushrooms in a dish and cover with the 125 mL (1/2 cup) hot water.
— Allow to soak for 30 minutes; remove the mushrooms and discard the water.
— Remove the mushroom caps; chop finely and set aside. Discard the stems.
— In a bowl, combine the ground pork, egg, soy sauce, salt and sugar, and mix well.

— Add the ginger, mushrooms, water chestnuts and green onion. Mix again.
— Shape into small meatballs, using 30 mL (2 tablespoons) of the meat mixture for each ball.
— Roll each ball in the cooked rice.
— Place the meatballs on a rack in a dish; add enough hot water to the

dish to cover the bottom.
— Cover and cook at 90%
  for 7 to 9 minutes, giving
  the dish a half-turn
  midway through the
  cooking time.
— Let stand for 2 minutes
  before serving.

*Here are all the ingredients
you will need to prepare this
very simple recipe.*

*After shaping the meatballs
with 30 mL (2 tablespoons) of
the meat mixture for each, roll
them in the cooked rice and
place on a rack in a dish.*

47

Ground Pork with Broccoli

Level of Difficulty	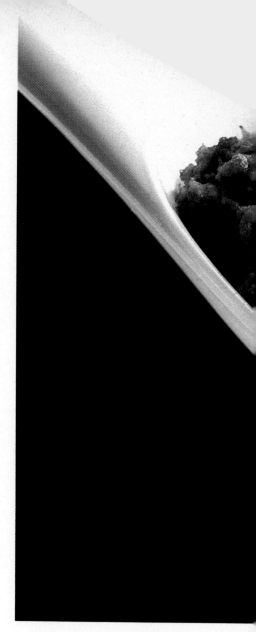
Preparation Time	15 min*
Cost per Serving	$ $
Number of Servings	2
Nutritional Value	286 calories 27.1 g protein 553 mg sodium
Food Exchanges	3 oz meat 1 vegetable exchange 1/2 fat exchange
Cooking Time	13 min
Standing Time	None
Power Level	100%
Write Your Cooking Time Here	

* The pork should be left to marinate for 20 minutes before cooking.

Ingredients
225 g (8 oz) lean ground pork
1 bunch broccoli
50 mL (1/4 cup) chicken broth
1 clove garlic, crushed

Marinade:
10 mL (2 teaspoons) fresh ginger root, chopped
30 mL (2 tablespoons) soy sauce
10 mL (2 teaspoons) sherry
5 mL (1 teaspoon) sesame oil
5 mL (1 teaspoon) cornstarch

Method
— In a bowl, combine the ingredients for the marinade and mix well.
— Add the ground pork and stir.
— Allow to marinate for 20 minutes.
— Meanwhile, cut up the broccoli; cut the flowerets into small pieces and slice the stalks into fine strips.
— Put the broccoli in a dish and add the chicken broth.
— Cover and cook for 4 to 5 minutes at 100%, but do not overcook; stir once during the cooking time, drain the broccoli and set aside. Reserve the cooking broth as well.
— Put the pork in a dish and add the garlic; cook for 4 to 5 minutes at 100%, breaking up the meat with a fork every 2 minutes.
— Add the broccoli and its cooking liquid to the meat and mix well.
— Cook the mixture at 100% for 2 to 3 minutes, stirring once during the cooking time.

This recipe is suitable for any occasion and can be prepared in a short time. Here are the ingredients needed to prepare it.

Allow the ground pork to soak in the marinade for 20 minutes.

Add the broccoli and the broth in which it was cooked to the pork before proceeding to the final cooking stage.

49

Pork Tenderloin Chiang Yu Wong

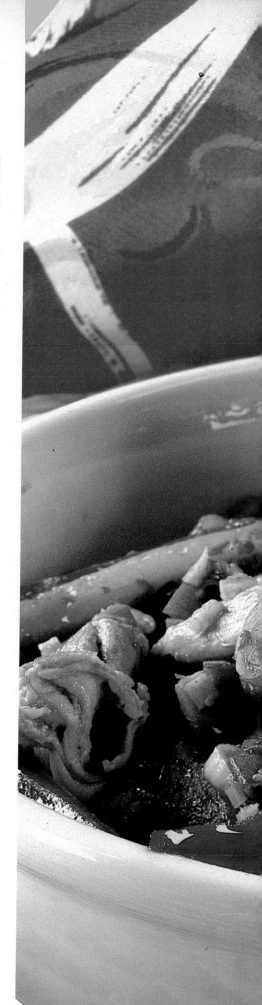

Level of Difficulty	▥▥ ▥▥
Preparation Time	30 min
Cost per Serving	$ $
Number of Servings	4
Nutritional Value	402 calories 25.9 g protein 4.2 mg iron
Food Exchanges	3 oz meat 1 vegetable exchange 3-1/2 fat exchanges
Cooking Time	5 min
Standing Time	4 min
Power Level	100%, 70%
Write Your Cooking Time Here	

Ingredients
450 g (1 lb) pork tenderloin
1 red pepper
2 dill pickles
1 piece ginger root, 3 cm
(1-1/4 in)
8 green onions
5 mL (1 teaspoon) cornstarch
7 mL (1/2 tablespoon) light
soy sauce
50 mL (1/4 cup) oil
7 mL (1/2 tablespoons) hot
soy paste (miso)

Sauce:
5 mL (1 teaspoon)
monosodium glutamate
5 mL (1 teaspoon) salt
5 mL (1 teaspoon) sugar
5 mL (1 teaspoon) white
vinegar

15 mL (1 tablespoon) light
soy sauce
2 mL (1/2 teaspoon) chili
sauce
30 mL (2 tablespoons) water
15 mL (1 tablespoon) sesame
oil

Method
— Cut the pork tenderloin
and the pepper into
strips; cut the pickles into
julienne strips, chop the
ginger and slice the
onions; set all these
ingredients aside.
— Dissolve the cornstarch in
the soy sauce, pour over
the pork and mix well; set
aside.

Pork Tenderloin Chiang Yu Wong

The delicacy of this dish makes it one of the most appreciated recipes in Chinese cooking. Here are the ingredients that are necessary to prepare it.

Cut the pork and the pepper into strips; cut the pickles into julienne strips; chop the ginger and slice the green onions.

Dissolve the cornstarch in the soy sauce, pour over the pork and mix well.

While the browning dish is heating, combine all the ingredients for the sauce in a bowl and mix well.

Once the vegetables have been seared, add the seared meat and the sauce to them.

Stir halfway through the cooking time to ensure uniform cooking.

— Preheat a browning dish for 7 minutes at 100%.
— Meanwhile, combine all the ingredients for the sauce in a bowl; mix well and set aside.
— Pour the oil into the browning dish and heat for 30 seconds at 100%.

— Sear the meat, remove and set aside.
— Put the browning dish back into the oven and heat for 3 minutes at 100%.
— Sear the peppers, pickles, green onions, ginger and soy paste.

— Add the meat and sauce.
— Cover the mixture and cook at 70% for 4 to 5 minutes, stirring once during the cooking.
— Let stand for 4 minutes and serve.

Pork Chop Suey

Ingredients
750 mL (3 cups) pork, cut
into strips
50 mL (1/4 cup) oil
250 mL (1 cup) onions, finely
chopped
250 mL (1 cup) green pepper,
cut into strips
500 mL (2 cups) celery, sliced
250 mL (1 cup) mushrooms,
sliced
900 g (2 lb) bean sprouts
1 284 mL (10 oz) can beef
consommé
45 mL (3 tablespoons) soy
sauce
30 mL (2 tablespoons)
cornstarch
5 mL (1 teaspoon) sugar
5 mL (1 teaspoon) salt

Method
— Preheat a browning dish
  for 7 minutes at 100%;
  add the oil and heat for
  30 seconds at 100%.
— Sear the strips of pork
  and add the onions,
  peppers and celery.
— Cover and cook at 100%
  for 3 to 4 minutes,
  stirring once during the
  cooking time.
— Add the mushrooms,
  cover again and continue
  cooking at 100% for 3 to
  4 minutes, stirring once
  during the cooking time.

— Add the bean sprouts,
  cover and set aside.
— In a bowl, combine the
  beef consommé with all
  the other ingredients; mix
  well.
— Add this mixture to the
  meat and vegetables.
— Cover and cook for 3 to
  4 minutes at 100%;
  stirring once each minute.
— Let stand for 5 minutes
  before serving.

Lobster with Mushrooms

Level of Difficulty	🍴🍴 🍴🍴
Preparation Time	20 min
Cost per Serving	$ $ $
Number of Servings	2
Nutritional Value	449 calories 22.9 g protein 23.7 mg iron
Food Exchanges	3.5 oz meat 2 vegetable exchanges 5 fat exchanges
Cooking Time	6 min
Standing Time	3 min
Power Level	100%, 90%
Write Your Cooking Time Here	

Ingredients
1 900 g (2 lb) lobster
1 340 g (12 oz) Chinese lettuce
6 large mushrooms
50 mL (1/4 cup) peanut oil

Sauce:
60 mL (4 tablespoons) soy sauce
15 mL (1 tablespoon) monosodium glutamate
30 mL (2 tablespoons) sake
5 mL (1 teaspoon) ginger extract
5 mL (1 teaspoon) sugar
5 mL (1 teaspoon) salt

Method
— Remove the meat from the lobster shell and cut into cubes; set aside.
— Tear the lettuce into pieces and cut the mushrooms in half; set aside.
— Preheat a browning dish for 7 minutes at 100%.
— Meanwhile, combine all the ingredients for the sauce in a bowl; mix well and set aside.
— Pour the oil into the browning dish and heat for 30 seconds at 100%.

— Sear the lobster meat and add the vegetables and sauce.
— Cover the dish; reduce the power to 90% and cook for 4 to 6 minutes, stirring once during the cooking time.
— Let stand for 3 minutes before serving.

Steamed Bass with Black Beans

Level of Difficulty	
Preparation Time	15 min
Cost per Serving	$
Number of Servings	4
Nutritional Value	265 calories 32.8 g protein 1.1 mg iron
Food Exchanges	4 oz meat
Cooking Time	9 min
Standing Time	3 min
Power Level	70%
Write Your Cooking Time Here	

Ingredients
2 bass, cleaned and trimmed
5 mL (1 teaspoon) fresh ginger root, finely chopped
1 green onion, sliced

Sauce:
15 mL (1 tablespoon) soy sauce
10 mL (2 teaspoons) salted black beans, chopped
15 mL (1 tablespoon) sake
15 mL (1 tablespoon) peanut oil
2 mL (1/2 teaspoon) sugar

Method
— Rinse the fish, inside and out, and dry carefully.
— Rub salt on the inside of the fish.
— With a knife, score the surface of the fish.
— Place the fish in a dish.
— In a bowl, mix all the ingredients for the sauce and pour over the fish.
— Sprinkle the fish with the ginger and green onions.
— Cover the dish; cook at 70% for 7 to 9 minutes or until the fish is cooked, giving the dish a half-turn midway through the cooking time.
— Let stand for 3 minutes before serving.

Here are the ingredients you must assemble before beginning to prepare this recipe.

With a sharp knife, score the surface of the fish.

After pouring the sauce over the fish, sprinkle with the ginger and green onions.

Shrimp Kiang

Level of Difficulty	
Preparation Time	15 min
Cost per Serving	$ $
Number of Servings	4
Nutritional Value	414 calories 27.7 g protein 3.4 mg iron
Food Exchanges	4 oz meat 2-1/2 fat exchanges
Cooking Time	5 min
Standing Time	3 min
Power Level	100%, 70%
Write Your Cooking Time Here	

Ingredients
450 g (1 lb) shrimp, peeled
45 mL (3 tablespoons) oil
250 mL (1 cup) cashew nuts
3 green onions, sliced
1 piece ginger root, 2.5 cm
(1 in), chopped

Sauce:
3 mL (3/4 teaspoon) wine
vinegar
2 mL (1/2 teaspoon) sugar
5 mL (1 teaspoon) cornstarch
dissolved in 15 mL
(1 tablespoon) water
30 mL (2 tablespoons)
tomato paste

Method

— Preheat a browning dish for 7 minutes at 100%.
— Meanwhile, place all the ingredients for the sauce in a bowl; mix well and set aside.
— Pour the oil into the browning dish and heat for 30 seconds at 100%.
— Sear the shrimp, add the nuts, green onions and ginger.
— Add the sauce and mix well.
— Cover and cook at 70% for 4 to 5 minutes, stirring once during the cooking time.
— Let stand for 3 minutes before serving.

MICROTIPS

Cooking Rice in the Microwave Oven

Rice, which has been a staple in the Orient for the past 5000 years, adapts very well to such modern cooking methods such as the microwave. The technique used is very similar to that used for cooking with a conventional stove. It will require a fairly long cooking time, from 15 to 35 minutes, depending on the quantity and type of rice used. Unlike most food cooked Chinese style in the microwave, rice requires a large quantity of water to cook properly. The exact amount of water and the total cooking time will vary with the type of rice used.

To cook long grain rice, place 500 mL (2 cups) of hot liquid and 250 mL (1 cup) of rice in a dish. Cover and bring to a boil by heating at 100% for 5 minutes. Reduce the power to 70% and continue cooking for 10 minutes.

Shrimp Kiang

Undoubtedly, you will enjoy shrimp prepared in this delightful way. Assemble the necessary ingredients before beginning this recipe.

Add the nuts, green onions and ginger to the seared shrimp.

Add the sauce to the shrimp, cashew nuts, green onions and ginger before proceeding to the final cooking stage.

MICROTIPS

Which Rice Should You Choose?

Here are a few useful facts about the varieties of rice we find in our supermarkets.

Long Grain, Medium Grain and Short Grain Rice

Don't make the mistake of thinking that all rice is classified according to its length. Not so. The terms long grain, medium grain and short grain correspond to precise varieties of rice or to a small number of closely related varieties. These terms are, in fact, a way of simplifying the classification of rice varieties.

Long grain rice is the lightest and yet the firmest of the three. The grains are flakier and have much less tendency to stick together than the shorter grained rices when cooked. It is the preferred variety when appearance is important and it is also often used for salads. Since the short and medium grain rices have a tendency to stick together when cooked, these varieties are used for dishes that call for rice cakes or for molded rice dishes. They are also used for stuffings and desserts. The type of rice is usually plainly marked on its package.

White Rice and Brown Rice

The difference between these two is that white rice has had the bran and germ removed. This refining process perhaps enhances the taste and texture of the rice but it removes several valuable nutrients. Brown rice, on the other hand, has a nutty flavor and a crunchy texture that many find appealing. It takes longer to cook than white rice.

Converted Rice

Converted rice is a compromise between white and brown rice in term of nutritional value. It is cooked under pressure in its natural state, before being polished. In this way the nutrients in the bran are forced into the core of the rice by steam pressure. The shell is then removed; the resulting rice is a little darker in color but its texture is similar to white rice.

Scallops Tsao Ku

Ingredients
450 g (1 lb) scallops
225 g (8 oz) Chinese
mushrooms

warm water
30 mL (2 tablespoons) flour
pepper to taste
50 mL (1/4 cup) oil

10 mL (2 teaspoons)
cornstarch dissolved in
30 mL (2 tablespoons) cold
water
50 mL (1/4 cup) chicken
broth
30 mL (2 tablespoons) soy
sauce

Level of Difficulty	🍴
Preparation Time	20 min*
Cost per Serving	$ $
Number of Servings	4
Nutritional Value	258 calories
21.9 g protein
480 mg sodium
Food Exchanges	3 oz meat
1 vegetable exchange
2-1/2 fat exchanges
Cooking Time	5 min
Standing Time	3 min
Power Level	100%
Write Your Cooking Time Here	

* Soak the Chinese mushrooms in warm water for 30 minutes before using.

Method
— Place the mushrooms in a bowl and cover with warm water; allow them to soak for 30 minutes.
— Drain the mushrooms; remove and discard the stems. Cut the caps into pieces about the same size as the scallops; set aside.
— Preheat a browning dish for 7 minutes at 100%.
— In the meantime, mix the flour and pepper, flour the scallops and set aside.
— Pour the oil into the browning dish and heat for 30 seconds at 100%.
— Sear the scallops and add the mushrooms and all the remaining ingredients.
— Cover and cook at 100% for 3 to 5 minutes, stirring each minute.
— Let stand for 3 minutes and serve.

Chinese Vegetables with Oyster Sauce

Level of Difficulty	
Preparation Time	30 min
Cost per Serving	**$**
Number of Servings	4
Nutritional Value	315 calories 36.8 g protein 2.8 mg iron
Food Exchanges	4 vegetable exchanges 1 bread exchange 3 fat exchanges
Cooking Time	10 min
Standing Time	3 min
Power Level	100%
Write Your Cooking Time Here	

Ingredients
1 red pepper
1 onion
1/2 head Chinese lettuce
125 mL (1/2 cup) water chestnuts
225 g (8 oz) mushrooms
250 mL (1 cup) bamboo shoots
500 mL (2 cups) canned baby corn on the cob
6 cloves garlic
225 g (8 oz) snow peas
50 mL (1/4 cup) oil
30 mL (2 tablespoons) cornstarch
250 mL (1 cup) cold chicken broth
50 mL (1/4 cup) oyster sauce

Method
— Slice the pepper, onion, lettuce, water chestnuts, mushrooms and bamboo shoots into strips.
— Cut the baby corn cobs in half lengthwise and crush the cloves of garlic.
— Preheat a browning dish for 7 minutes at 100%. Add the oil and heat for 30 seconds at 100%.
— Sear all the vegetables and the garlic; cover and cook at 100% for 4 to 5 minutes, stirring once during the cooking time, and set aside.
— Mix the cornstarch and chicken broth; add the oyster sauce and mix well.
— Cook the sauce at 100% for 3 to 5 minutes or until it thickens, stirring twice during the cooking time.
— Pour the sauce over the vegetables and mix well.
— Cover and let stand for 3 minutes before serving.

All these ingredients come together in a dish that is a harmony of color and flavor—one of the delights of oriental cuisine.

Pour the sauce over the seared vegetables and stir to mix well. Cover and let stand for 3 minutes.

MICROTIPS

To Open Oysters

Holding the oyster firmly with a folded cloth (to protect your hand) on a flat surface, slide the point of an oyster knife into the small opening between the shells and twist the blade. With this twisting motion, work the knife further in between the shells to cut the ligament; then remove the upper shell.

Trout Mi-Chiu

Level of Difficulty	
Preparation Time	15 min
Cost per Serving	$ $
Number of Servings	2
Nutritional Value	350 calories 32.4 g protein 3.3 mg iron
Food Exchanges	4.5 oz meat 1 vegetable exchange
Cooking Time	6 min
Standing Time	3 min
Power Level	70%
Write Your Cooking Time Here	

Ingredients

2 trout, cleaned and trimmed
8 thin slices ginger root, cut into strips
8 mushrooms, sliced
6 green onions, sliced

Glaze:
15 mL (1 tablespoon) sake
5 mL (1 teaspoon) sugar
5 mL (1 teaspoon) cornstarch
15 mL (1 tablespoon) soy sauce

Method

— In a bowl, combine the ingredients for the glaze and mix well.
— Place the trout in a dish and brush the inside of each with a very small amount of the glaze.
— Brush the remaining glaze over the trout and sprinkle with the ginger, mushrooms and green onions.
— Cover and cook at 70% for 4 to 6 minutes or until the fish is done. The trout is cooked when the flesh crumbles easily with a fork.
— Let stand for 3 minutes before standing.

Sauces for a Harmonious Cuisine

The search for harmony in culinary art is the fundamental principle of oriental cooking. Dishes must not only taste good, they must also be balanced in terms of the various ingredients in their composition. The ancient art of Chinese cooking depends on the contrast of flavors, colors and textures. In meal plans you will see a constant alternation between crunchy dishes and creamy ones, and a spicy preparation always accompanies bland dishes. Following the same principle, dishes with little color will always be enhanced by a fruit or vegetable or another dish with a strong, bright color.

One can easily see, then, that sauces would enjoy an important role in this search for harmony. They can be used to heighten the milk taste of a given dish or perhaps to temper the strong flavor of a particular food. Sweet sauces present a delicious contrast when served with salty foods and soften the taste of food that is spicy or vinegary. Sauces also provide a whole gamut of colors and textures that enable chefs to embellish their dishes.

It would be difficult, in just a few lines, to deal with the hundreds of sauces that have been developed over the centuries of oriental cooking. This being the case, we will deal with just a few representatives.

First, let us look at those sauces that are readily available in our markets. Without doubt, the best known is soy sauce, which has been in use since at least 500 BC. It can be used as a condiment at the table or as a flavoring agent in the preparation of many dishes. Plum sauce and cherry sauce are equally popular in Western countries and are a perfect foil for salty dishes. Hoisin sauce, a sweet, spicy vegetable sauce, is especially good as a dip for fish, seafood or poultry. Finally, oyster sauce, a Cantonese speciality, is without equal when you want to enhance the flavor of meats, vegetables or seafood.

The variety of oriental sauces is almost limitless. For this volume, we have chosen three sauces that will complement many dishes: a plum sauce, a lichee sauce and a red sauce, as lemony and vinegary as you could wish for.

One can easily see, then, that sauces would enjoy an important role in this search for harmony. They can be used to heighten the mild taste of a given dish or perhaps to temper the strong flavor of a particular food. Sweet sauces present a delicious contrast when served with salty foods and soften the taste of food that is spicy or vinegary. Sauces also provide a whole gamut of colors and textures that enable chefs to embellish their dishes.

Plum Sauce

Level of Difficulty	🍴
Preparation Time	5 min*
Cost per Serving	$
Number of Servings	About 250 mL (1 cup) or 8 servings, 30 mL (2 tablespoons) each
Nutritional Value	50 calories 0.2 g protein 0.5 mg iron
Food Exchanges	1 fruit exchange
Cooking Time	6 min
Standing Time	None
Power Level	100%
Write Your Cooking Time Here	

* This sauce should be refrigerated before serving.

Ingredients
1 398 mL (14 oz) can plums, with their syrup
30 mL (2 tablespoons) vinegar
15 mL (1 tablespoon) brown sugar
15 mL (1 tablespoon) onion, grated
5 mL (1 teaspoon) red pimento, crushed
1 clove garlic, sliced
2 mL (1/2 teaspoon) fresh ginger root, finely chopped

Method
— In a bowl, combine all the ingredients and mix well.
— Cook at 100% for 6 minutes, stirring twice during the cooking time.
— Allow to cool.
— Pour the sauce into a blender and mix for a few seconds to obtain a smooth consistency.
— Keep the sauce in the refrigerator and serve with your favorite dishes.

Assemble all the ingredients necessary for this remarkable sauce, one that is always useful to have on hand.

MICROTIPS

Leftover Sauces For Making . . . Sauces!
Sauces, whether in Chinese cooking or in our own Western cooking, lend their flavors and aromas to the dishes with which they are served. One of the secrets of Chinese cooking rests in the art of renewing sauces. First, it is highly

recommended that all juices from the cooking of meat, poultry or fish be saved. With water and seasonings added, they can be used to cook other foods and to make sauces.

This process of creating sauces from re-used meat juices, cooking liquids or sauces

previously made can carry on indefinitely. The greater the variety of food a sauce is cooked with, the more flavor it will acquire. Some experts say that some sauces are preserved by Chinese families for several years, while others claim they endure for generations!

Lichee Sauce

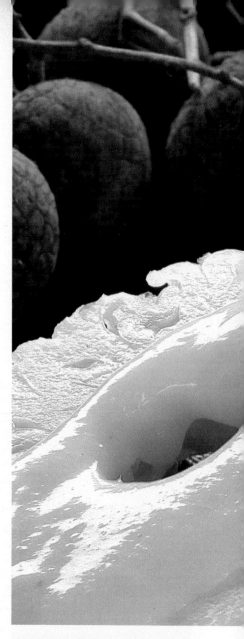

Level of Difficulty	🍴🍴
Preparation Time	5 min*
Cost per Serving	$
Number of Servings	Appoximately 500 mL (2 cups) or 16 servings, 30 mL (2 tablespoons) each
Nutritional Value	25 calories 0.1 g protein 2.7 mg carbohydrate
Food Exchanges	1/2 fruit exchange
Cooking Time	3 min
Standing Time	None
Power Level	100%
Write Your Cooking Time Here	🍎✏️

* This sauce should be served at room temperature.

Ingredients
1 540 mL (19 oz) can lichees
15 mL (1 tablespoon) cornstarch
15 mL (1 tablespoon) cold water
15 mL (1 tablespoon) candied ginger
30 mL (2 tablespoons) butter
45 mL (3 tablespons) lime juice
zest from 1 lime, blanched

Method
— Drain the lichees, set aside and save the liquid.
— Dissolve the cornstarch in the cold water and add it to the lichee juice.
— Cook for 3 minutes at 100%, stirring every minute.
— Add the other ingredients and put in a blender; blend at high speed for a few seconds to obtain a smooth consistency.
— Pass the sauce through a fine sieve.
— Allow to cool and serve at room temperature.

Mixed with the other ingredients, the characteristic flavor of the lichees will be enhanced.

Dissolve the cornstarch in cold water and add to the lichee juice.

Cook for 3 minutes at 100%, stirring every minute.

Add all the other ingredients and blend at high speed in a blender for a few seconds to obtain a smooth consistency.

Red Sauce

Level of Difficulty	🍴
Preparation Time	5 min*
Cost per Serving	**$**
Number of Servings	About 750 mL (3 cup) or 24 servings, 30 mL (2 tablespoons) each
Nutritional Value	64 calories 16.4 g carbohydrate
Food Exchanges	1 fruit exchange
Cooking Time	4 min
Standing Time	None
Power Level	100%
Write Your Cooking Time Here	✏️🍎

* This sauce should be refrigerated before serving. Note that it can be kept up to 1 month in the refrigerator.

Ingredients
175 mL (3/4 cup) ketchup
125 mL (1/2 cup) vinegar
175 mL (3/4 cup) water
400 mL (1-2/3 cups) sugar
30 mL (2 tablespoons) lemon juice
30 mL (2 tablespoons) cornstarch dissolved in 50 mL (1/4 cup) cold water

Method
— In a bowl, combine all the ingredients except the cornstarch and cold water; mix well.
— Cook for 2 minutes at 100%, stirring once during the cooking time.
— Add the dissolved cornstarch and stir.
— Cook for 2 minutes at 100%, stirring once during the cooking time.
— Allow to cool before serving with your favorite dishes.

Assemble all the ingredients required to make this outstanding sauce.

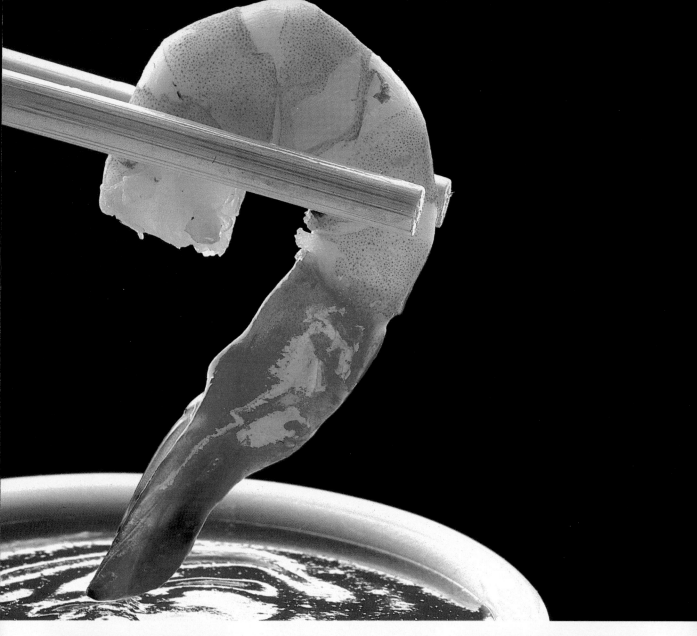

In a large bowl, combine all the ingredients for the sauce except the cornstarch and cold water, and mix well.

Cook the mixture for 2 minutes at 100%, stirring once during the cooking time.

Add the dissolved cornstarch to the mixture. Cook for 2 minutes at 100%, stirring midway through the cooking time.

Fried Rice with Soy Sauce

Level of Difficulty	⚮
Preparation Time	15 min
Cost per Serving	$
Number of Servings	4
Nutritional Value	263 calories 1.6 g protein 1337 mg sodium
Food Exchanges	1 bread exchange 3 fat exchanges
Cooking Time	23 min
Standing Time	None
Power Level	100%, 70%
Write Your Cooking Time Here	

Ingredients
250 mL (1 cup) long grain white rice
500 mL (2 cups) hot water
10 mL (2 teaspoons) salt
50 mL (1/4 cup) oil
45 mL (3 tablespoons) soy sauce
60 mL (4 tablespoons) brown sugar
50 mL (1/4 cup) green onions, sliced

Method
— Pour the water into a dish and add half the salt and rice.
— Cover and cook for 5 minutes at 100%.
— Reduce the power to 70% and continue to cook for 10 minutes.
— Stir the rice and set aside.
— In a bowl, mix the oil, soy sauce, brown sugar and remaining salt; whisk well to obtain a smooth consistency.
— Add this sauce to the rice and mix well.
— Arrange the rice on a large serving platter.
— Without covering cook for 6 to 8 minutes at 100%; stirring every 2 minutes.
— Garnish with the uncooked green onions and serve.

Tsung Fried Rice

Level of Difficulty	(icon)
Preparation Time	20 min
Cost per Serving	$
Number of Servings	4
Nutritional Value	434 calories 24.3 g protein 4.2 mg iron
Food Exchanges	2.5 oz meat 1/2 vegetable exchange 2 bread exchanges 2-1/2 fat exchanges
Cooking Time	11 min
Standing Time	2 min
Power Level	100%
Write Your Cooking Time Here	(icon)

Ingredients
750 mL (3 cups) rice, cooked
3 eggs
45 mL (3 tablespoons) milk
125 mL (1/2 cup) frozen
green peas
50 mL (1/4 cup) oil
250 mL (1 cup) meat of your
choice, cooked and diced
2 clove garlic, crushed
250 mL (1 cup) shrimp,
cooked
5 mL (1 teaspoon) salt
3 mL (3/4 teaspoon)
monosodium glutamate
15 mL (1 tablespoon) sake
50 mL (1/4 cup) green
onions, sliced

Method
— In a small bowl, combine
  the eggs and milk and
  mix well; cook at 100%
  for 3 to 5 minutes,
  stirring every minute, and
  set aside.
— Place the peas in a dish,
  cover and cook for 2 to 3
  minutes at 100%; stirring
  once during the cooking
  time and set aside.
— Preheat a browning dish
  for 7 minutes at 100%;
  pour the oil into the dish
  and heat for 30 seconds
  at 100%.
— Add the rice, meat and
  garlic, and stir rapidly.
— Add the shrimp, peas,
  salt, monosodium
  glutamate and the sake,
  and stir well.
— Without covering cook
  for 2 minutes at 100%.
— Add the egg and the milk
  mixture, and mix well.
— Cook for 1 minute at
  100%.
— Garnish with the
  uncooked green onions
  and let stand for 2
  minutes before serving.

Assemble these ingredients to produce a rice dish that is perfect for all occasions.

Cook the egg and milk mixture at 100% for 3 to 5 minutes, stirring every minute.

Add the shrimp, peas, salt, monosodium glutamate and sake to the fried rice mixture and stir before proceeding with the cooking.

Fried Rice with Ham and Eggs

Level of Difficulty	🍴
Preparation Time	15 min
Cost per Serving	$
Number of Servings	4
Nutritional Value	340 calories 19.6 g protein 1027 mg sodium
Food Exchanges	2.5 oz meat 1/2 bread exchange 2 fat exchanges
Cooking Time	8 min
Standing Time	None
Power Level	100%
Write Your Cooking Time Here	

Ingredients
250 mL (1 cup) rice, cooked
75 mL (1/3 cup) frozen green peas
2 eggs, lightly beaten
50 mL (1/4 cup) oil
2 slices ham, 0.5 cm (1/4 in) thick, diced
5 mL (1 teaspoon) salt
1 green onion, sliced

Method
— Place the peas in a dish, cover and cook for 3 minutes at 100%; drain and set aside.
— Cook the beaten eggs at 100% for 2 to 3 minutes, stirring once during the cooking time; set aside.
— Preheat a browning dish for 7 minutes at 100%; add the oil and heat for 30 seconds at 100%.
— Sear the rice and ham; add the salt.
— Add the peas, cooked eggs and green onion; mix well.
— Cook the entire mixture at 100% for 2 minutes, stirring once during the cooking time.
— Serve immediately.

Cooked rice, eggs, diced ham, frozen green peas, oil, salt and sliced green onion—all the ingredients needed for an extraordinary rice dish!

In a preheated browning dish add the oil and heat; sear the rice and ham and add the salt.

Add the peas, cooked eggs and green onion to the rice and ham. Mix well before the final stage of cooking.

Cook the entire mixture for 2 minutes at 100%; stir halfway through the cooking time.

Chicken and Rice Casserole

Level of Difficulty	🍴
Preparation Time	15 min
Cost per Serving	$
Number of Servings	4
Nutritional Value	140 calories 11.4 g protein 561 mg sodium
Food Exchanges	1 oz meat 1 bread exchange
Cooking Time	22 min
Standing Time	5 min
Power Level	100%
Write Your Cooking Time Here	

Ingredients
150 mL (2/3 cup) chicken, cooked and diced
250 mL (1 cup) long grain white rice
500 mL (2 cups) chicken broth
5 mL (1 teaspoon) salt
75 mL (1/3 cup) kohlrabi, sliced
150 mL (2/3 cup) Chinese lettuce, shredded

Method
— Pour the chicken broth into a dish; bring to a boil by heating for 8 to 10 minutes at 100%.
— Add the rice and salt.
— Cover and cook for 10 to 12 minutes at 100%.
— Add the chicken and the vegetables; mix well.
— Cover and let stand for 5 minutes before serving.

Without a doubt, your day-to-day meals will be more interesting when you serve this dish, so easy to prepare.

Add the rice and salt to the hot chicken broth; cover and cook for 10 to 12 minutes at 100%.

Add the chicken and vegetables to the rice. Cover and allow to stand for 5 minutes before serving.

MICROTIPS

Instant Rice: What Is It?

Instant rice is a white rice that has been cooked and then dehydrated. Although vitamin and mineral content, the flavor and the texture all suffer from this process, the speed with which it can be prepared makes it a popular convenience item.

Corn Soup

Ingredients

1 540 mL (19 oz) can
cream–style corn
1 whole chicken breast
1.25 L (5 cups) chicken broth

45 mL (3 tablespoons)
cornstarch dissolved in
50 mL (1/4 cup) water
2 egg yolks
15 mL (1 tablespoon) oil

Level of Difficulty	🍴
Preparation Time	20 min*
Cost per Serving	$
Number of Servings	8
Nutritional Value	122 calories 6.9 g protein 0.6 mg iron
Food Exchanges	0.5 oz meat 2 vegetable exchanges 1/2 fat exchange
Cooking Time	21 min
Standing Time	5 min
Power Level	70%, 100%
Write Your Cooking Time Here	✏️

Method

— Cook the chicken breast
for 7 to 9 minutes at
70%; give the dish a
half-turn midway
through the cooking time.
— Allow the chicken to
cool; remove the meat
from the bones, cut into
strips and set aside.
— Heat the chicken broth
for 7 to 9 minutes at
100%; stir once.
— Add the corn and
dissolved cornstarch to
the broth.
— Beat the egg yolks with
the oil and add to the
soup, stirring constantly.
— Cook at 100% for 2 to 3
minutes, stirring each
minute. Do not allow the
soup to boil.
— Add the strips of chicken
and let stand for 5
minutes before serving.

* Allow the chicken breast to cool before removing the meat from the
bones and cutting it into strips.

82

Chicken Soup with Snow Peas

Ingredients

750 mL (3 cups) white meat of chicken, diced
250 mL (1 cup) snow peas

250 mL (1 cup) carrots, cut in julienne strips
2.25 L (9 cups) water
12 mL (2-1/2 teaspoons) salt

12 mL (2-1/2 teaspoons) monosodium glutamate
3 mL (3/4 teaspoon) sugar
30 mL (2 tablespoons) white wine
5 mL (1 teaspoon) pepper

Level of Difficulty	🍴
Preparation Time	20 min
Cost per Serving	$
Number of Servings	12
Nutritional Value	75 calories 12.7 g protein 0.6 mg iron
Food Exchanges	1 oz meat 1/2 vegetable exchange
Cooking Time	37 min
Standing Time	5 min
Power Level	100%
Write Your Cooking Time Here	

Method
— Place the snow peas and carrots in a dish; add 50 mL (1/4 cup) of the water.
— Cover and cook for 5 to 6 minutes at 100%, stirring once; drain and set aside.
— Bring the remaining water to a boil in a casserole by heating for 14 to 16 minutes at 100%.
— Add the chicken and all the other ingredients except the snow peas and carrots.
— Continue to cook at 100% for 10 to 15 minutes.
— Add the cooked snow peas and carrots to the soup.
— Let stand for 5 minutes before serving.

83

When East and West Meet for Dessert

What do Orientals eat for dessert? Anyone who has not made a study of oriental cuisine might indeed wonder. A few run–of–the–mill confections such as almond cookies or fortune cookies come to mind.

Unfortunately, these desserts, as we know them, are usually local adaptations of oriental foods. A survey of menus in Asiatic restaurants does not make anyone the wiser. Unless you happen to find a restaurant that has really adapted to Western tastes, you will generally find very few pastries or desserts on the menu. Do the oriental people dislike sugar? Not at all, judging by the enthusiasm Chinese children show for barley sugar! Generally speaking, it is usually between meals, rather than for dessert at the end of a meal, that the adults will indulge in something sweet. Their preferences are for spicy preparations such as spring rolls or perhaps some dried fruit or a few cookies. Not a pastry in sight!

However, oriental desserts must exist! Historical accounts of feasts prepared for the nobility describe, among other things, whipped cream flavored with a chestnut puree and surrounded by candied pecans. Chinese desserts really do exist, but they are not normally part of everyday meals as in the Western world. In China, desserts are served only on festive occasions. They are usually presented midway through the meal as a break from the succession of savory dishes being served. This tradition is quite foreign to Westerners, who would have difficulty with a sweet course that is not served at the end of the meal.

On the following pages, we have assembled a few recipes for oriental desserts that are somewhat similar to our own. But we realize that fruit served with tea would probably be received more enthusiastically by our Chinese friends than these sweet desserts, which are nonetheless authentic. Let us consider each of these desserts as a delicious meeting point of Eastern and Western cultures.

Hzing Zen Jelly

Level of Difficulty	🍴🍴 🍴🍴
Preparation Time	20 min*
Cost per Serving	$ $
Number of Servings	6
Nutritional Value	188 calories 40.8 g carbohydrate 108.5 mg calcium
Food Exchanges	2 fruit exchanges 1/2 milk exchange
Cooking Time	5 min
Standing Time	None
Power Level	100%
Write Your Cooking Time Here	🍎✏️

* Let the molds containing the jellied fruit set at room temperature for 30 minutes, then refrigerate for 4 hours before serving.

Ingredients
2 envelopes unflavored gelatin
75 mL (1/3 cup) cold water
500 mL (2 cups) milk
150 mL (2/3 cup) sugar
15 mL (1 tablespoon) almond extract
125 mL (1/2 cup) canned pineapple, cut into cubes and drained
125 mL (1/2 cup) peaches, cut into cubes and drained
125 mL (1/2 cup) pears, cut into cubes and drained
50 mL (1/4 cup) red cherries, cut in two and drained
50 mL (1/4 cup) green cherries, cut in two and drained

Method
— Sprinkle the surface of the water with the gelatin; set aside.
— Pour the milk into a bowl and heat for 4 to 5 minutes at 100%; do not allow it to boil.
— Add the sugar to the milk; add the gelatin and water and stir.
— Add the almond extract and the fruit; mix well.
— Run six molds under cold tap water and then fill each with equal amounts of the mixture.
— Let sit at room temperature for 30 minutes and then refrigerate for 4 hours.
— Unmold the individual portions of the jelly and serve.

This dessert makes a refreshing finishing touch to a good meal. Here are the ingredients needed to succeed with this recipe.

Sprinkle the gelatin on the surface of the water in order to soften it.

Heat the milk for 4 to 5 minutes at 100% but do not allow it to boil.

Almond Cookies

Level of Difficulty	🍴🍴
Preparation Time	20 min*
Cost per Serving	$
Number of Servings	24 cookies
Nutritional Value	61 calories 1 g protein 6.9 g carbohydrate
Food Exchanges	1/2 bread exchange 1/2 fat exchange
Cooking Time	3 min
Standing Time	None
Power Level	70%
Write Your Cooking Time Here	

* Refrigerate the cookie dough for 3 hours before cooking.

Ingredients
50 mL (1/4 cup) lard
125 mL (1/2 cup) sugar
1 egg
7 mL (1/2 tablespoon) almond extract
4 drops yellow food coloring
175 mL (3/4 cup) flour
2 mL (1/2 teaspoon) baking soda
1 mL (1/4 teaspoon) salt
12 almonds, cut in half and toasted

Method
— In a bowl, cream the lard and sugar until light and fluffy.
— Add the egg, almond extract and food coloring; mix well and set aside.
— Sift the flour, baking soda and salt; add to the creamed mixture and knead only as long as necessary to blend, but not to toughen, the dough.
— Shape the dough into a long cylinder.
— Cover with plastic wrap and refrigerate for 3 hours.
— Cut the roll of dough into 24 slices, not more than 0.5 cm (1/4 in) thick.
— Place 12 slices of the cookie dough on a rack, press one almond half into each.
— Place on a raised rack in the microwave oven and cook for 1-1/2 minutes at 70%; give the rack a half–turn midway through the cooking time.
— Repeat the process for the remaining 12 slices.

Light and delicious, these cookies can be served as a snack as well for dessert. Assemble all the ingredients required to prepare them.

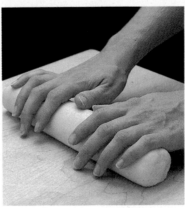

Shape the cookie dough into a long cylinder.

Cut the roll of dough into 24 slices, 0.5 cm (1/4 in) each in width.

Lichee Mousse

Level of Difficulty	▟▛ ▟▛
Preparation Time	20 min*
Cost per Serving	$ $
Number of Servings	8
Nutritional Value	120 calories 11.5 g protein 11.7 g carbohydrate
Food Exchanges	1 oz meat 1 fruit exchange
Cooking Time	3 min
Standing Time	None
Power Level	100%
Write Your Cooking Time Here	

* Refrigerate the mousse for 4 hours before serving.

Ingredients
1 540 mL (19 oz) can lichees
30 mL (2 tablespoons) unflavored gelatin
90 mL (6 tablespoons) cold water
2 squares tofu, 450 g (1 lb) total, drained
2 kiwis, sliced

Method
— Carefully drain the lichees and reserve the juice. Set aside.
— Sprinkle the surface of the water with gelatin and set aside for 3 to 5 minutes to soften.
— Pour the lichee juice into a bowl and heat for 2 to 3 minutes at 100%; do not allow it to boil.
— Add the gelatin to the lichee juice and stir until completely dissolved; allow to cool.
— Combine the tofu, lichees and juice mixture and place in a blender; blend for a few seconds until the consistency is smooth.
— Divide half the mixture equally among eight dessert cups and add a slice of kiwi to each. Distribute the remaining half equally among the cups and garnish each serving with the remaining kiwi slices.
— Refrigerate for 4 hours before serving.

MICROTIPS

To Remove the Skin from Almonds

Almonds are covered with a skin that is rather bitter tasting. To remove the skin first soften it by blanching the almonds, that is, by placing them in boiling water for approximately 1 minute. Drain the almonds in a strainer and spread them out on a cloth on a flat surface. Fold the cloth over the almonds and rub until all the skins have been removed.

To Break Open A Coconut

If not done properly, breaking open a coconut can be a hazardous procedure. Here is a sure-fire method of going about it:

1. Collect the milk:
Puncture the "eyes" (the soft parts) with a punch and drain the milk into a bowl.

2. Split the outer shell:
Hold the coconut firmly in one hand. Holding it straight, hit around the crown with the blunt side of a butcher knife. Then cut out a kind of lid.

3. Peel the outer shell:
With a knife, remove the brown outer hull that covers the meat of the coconut.

4. Grate the coconut meat:
Grate the coconut meat with a fine grater.

Coconut Tarts

Level of Difficulty	🍴🍴
Preparation Time	30 min*
Cost per Serving	**S**
Number of Servings	12 tarts
Nutritional Value	80 calories 3.4 g protein 25.4 g carbohydrate
Food Exchanges	1 fruit exchange 1 bread exchange 1 fat exchange
Cooking Time	5 min
Standing Time	None
Power Level	100%
Write Your Cooking Time Here	

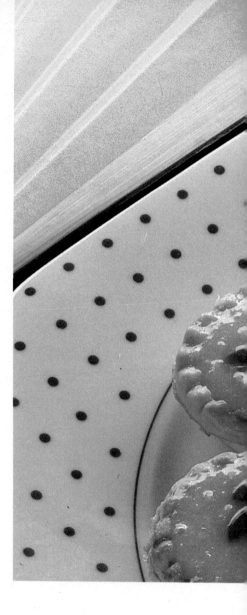

* Allow the filling to cool before pouring into the tart shells.

Ingredients
12 tart shells, baked
150 mL (2/3 cup) sugar
125 mL (1/2 cup) boiling
water
45 mL (3 tablespoons) butter
2 eggs, beaten
5 mL (1 teaspoon) milk
a few drops vanilla extract
2 mL (1/2 teaspoon) baking
powder
125 mL (1/2 cup) coconut,
grated
6 cherries, sliced

Method
— Dissolve the sugar in the
boiling water by heating
for 3 minutes at 100%,
stirring twice during the
cooking times.
— Add the butter and stir;
set aside.
— In a bowl, combine the
beaten eggs, milk, vanilla,
baking powder and
coconut, and mix well.
— Add the sugar mixture;
mix well to obtain a
smooth consistency.
— Cook the entire mixture
for 2 minutes at 100%;
stir twice during the
cooking time and allow to
cool.
— Pour an equal amount of
the filling into each tart
shell and garnish with the
cherry slices.

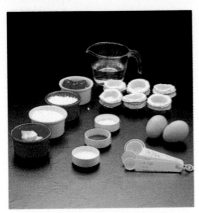

Here are the ingredients required for the preparation of these delicious coconut tarts.

Dissolve the sugar in the boiling water by heating for 3 minutes at 100%; stir twice during the cooking time.

Pour the dissolved sugar and butter into the mixture of eggs, milk, vanilla, baking powder and coconut. Cook at 100% for 2 minutes, stirring twice.

Ententaining

Menu:
Winter Melon Soup
Lotus Root Salad
Beef and Peppers
Steamed Rice

There is no need to make the long trek to China nor to stand in lineups at the more popular Chinese restaurants in order to enjoy fine oriental cuisine. You will now be able to prepare a thousand and one exotic creations at home that will amaze and delight your guests.

Thanks to the directions and recipes in this volume you will be able to serve veritable feasts, worthy of the greatest Chinese chefs. And what is more, you won't have to resort to dressing up in silk to convince your friends of the authenticity of your meal—it will stand on its own merit!

Since the Chinese, gastronomic magicians and guardians of the long tradition that they are, excel in the preparation of unlimited dishes, we offer here a menu for entertaining that is typical of their varied cuisine.

Light and refreshing, the winter melon (Tong-Kow) soup will delight the most discriminating of palates. The lotus root salad, with its subtle aroma, will balance harmoniously with the beef and peppers, a dish that the gourmets among you will rave about for a long time. Of course, this delicious meal will also include white rice, a traditional accompaniment to any Chinese meal.

"But what about dessert?" asks our anxious hostess. According to tradition none is required—and no one will really miss it, you may be sure. Bon appetit!

From the Recipe to Your Table

Planning a meal for company requires organization. A meal cooked in the microwave oven requires the same amount of planning as one cooked in a conventional oven. Only the cooking and reheating times are different.

6 hours before the meal:
—Marinate the beef.
2 hours before the meal:
—Prepare the winter melon soup.
1 hour and 30 minutes before the meal:
—Prepare the lotus root salad.
40 minutes before the meal:
—Prepare the steamed rice.
25 minutes before the meal:
—Cook the beef.

Winter Melon Soup

Ingredients
1 winter melon
6 fragrant mushrooms
125 mL (1/2 cup) warm water
500 mL (2 cups) chicken broth
50 mL (1/4 cup) ham, cut into fine strips

Method
— Place the mushrooms in a bowl, cover with the warm water and set aside for 30 minutes.
— Drain the mushrooms.
— Remove the stems and discard; chop the mushroom caps coarsely.
— Cut the melon into cubes.

— Heat the chicken broth for 5 to 6 minutes at 100%; add the melon cubes and mushrooms.
— Cook at 100% for 6 to 8 minutes, stirring once during the cooking time.
— Garnish with the strips of ham and serve.

Lotus Root Salad

Ingredients
450 g (1 lb) fresh lotus roots
1 L (4 cups) water
15 mL (1 tablespoon) soy sauce
15 mL (1 tablespoon) sake
15 mL (1 tablespoon) sugar
7 mL (1/2 tablespoon) oil
2 mL (1/2 teaspoon) salt

Method
— Rinse the lotus roots and peel.
— Cut the roots into thin slices, place in a dish and set aside.
— Bring the water to a boil by heating for 8 to 10 minutes at 100%.
— Pour the boiling water over the lotus root slices and let them soak.
— Pour the boiling water

over the lotus root slices and let them soak for 5 minutes; drain and dry well.
— In a bowl, combine the soy sauce, sake, sugar, oil and salt, and stir until the sugar and salt are dissolved.
— Pour the dressing over the slices of lotus and refrigerate for 1 hour before serving.

Beef and Peppers

Level of Difficulty	
Preparation Time	20 min*
Cost per Serving	$ $
Number of Servings	4
Nutritional Value	332 calories 27.8 g protein 3.5 mg iron
Food Exchanges	3 oz meat 1/2 vegetable exchange 2-1/2 fat exchanges
Cooking Time	5 min
Standing Time	3 min
Power Level	100%, 70%
Write Your Cooking Time Here	

* The meat should be marinated in the refrigerator for 5 hours before cooking.

Method
— In a dish, mix all the ingredients for the marinade.
— Cut the beef into strips and marinate them in the refrigerator for 5 hours.
— Cut the peppers into fine strips and set aside.
— Remove the beef from the marinade; set the marinade aside.
— Preheat a browning dish for 7 minutes at 100%; add the oil and heat for 30 seconds at 100%.
— Sear the strips of beef, remove and set aside.
— Reheat the browning dish for 3 minutes at 100%.
— Sear the strips of pepper and ginger.
— Add the beef, the remaining marinade and the dissolved cornstarch.
— Let stand for 3 minutes before serving.

Ingredients
450 g (1 lb) beef tenderloin
1 green pepper
1 red pepper
50 mL (1/4 cup) oil
4 slices fresh ginger root
10 mL (2 teaspoons)
cornstarch dissolved in
30 mL (2 tablespoons) cold
water

Marinade:
15 mL (1 tablespoon) sake
45 mL (3 tablespoons) soy
sauce
5 mL (1 teaspoon) sugar

Steamed Rice

Ingredients
250 mL (1 cup) white rice
500 mL (2 cups) hot water
5 mL (1 teaspoon) salt

Method
— Put the rice, hot water and salt into a casserole.
— Cover and cook for 5 minutes at 100%.
— Reduce the power to 70% and continue to cook for 10 minutes.
— Let stand for 5 minutes, divide into 4 equal portions and serve.

Preparing a Chinese Meal

The fundamental principles of oriental cuisine are based on a philosophy rooted in antiquity and passed on to the people of these countries by their scholars. A study of the writings of Confucius, the most well-known of the Chinese philosophers, will reveal a belief in a link between the mind and the senses, including the gastronomic.

In the Chinese philosophy, harmony is of prime importance and this cuisine from the other side of the world, is famous for some surprising combinations. Foods that we in the West would never think of combining are transformed by these culinary magicians into harmonious creations. But, also in the name of harmony, they believe that certain ingredients should never be combined because their flavors or nutrients are incompatible. The Chinese regard life as a natural duality, a balance of conflicting elements. They have applied the principles of Yin (feminine and somber) and Yang (masculine and light), two aspects of reality that are at once complementary and contradictory, to their cooking. This Taoist religious philosophy dates back several centuries BC and has flourished in the Far East. But it is hardly necessary to be an expert in oriental philosophies to appreciate their influence on the art of Chinese cooking.

As in any field of endeavor, cooking is best organized in stages and will succeed only when certain basic rules are observed. Our Asiatic friends have a few simple rules that necessitate a certain amount of organization. Chinese cooks are noted for being methodical and also for being very concerned about cleanliness. While they expect various flavors to intermingle during cooking, they are very fussy about rinsing their knives and cleavers often during the preparation of a meal; for example, bits of fish remaining on a knife blade must never be allowed to mix with meat that is to be cut up.

Cooking

When you are ready to cook, several methods are available to you. As we have said before, certain meats such as pork benefit from marinating for several hours, or even several days, before being sautéed or roasted. Although ingredients that are moist cook more quickly in the microwave it is important, for proper sautéing or searing, for meat that has been marinated to be carefully drained and wiped dry before cooking. Because the majority of Chinese dishes call for rapid cooking, the characteristics of the modern microwave oven are the perfect answer to this requirement of the ancient art of Chinese cookery.

In order to avoid overcooking, you must add the various ingredients in a certain order, depending on the amount of time required for each. The success of a recipe greatly depends on proper procedure at this stage of cooking. You must also make sure that the ingredients, whether meat, fish or vegetables, are cut into pieces of equal size for even cooking.

Cooking methods with the modern microwave do not require the same constant attention as those with the conventional stove because the cooking times are set in advance. But some attention is necessary because Chinese cooking requires stirring at intervals to ensure even sautéing of all ingredients.

If you are using liquids such as a court bouillon to poach fish or a chicken stock for poultry, Chinese cooks recommend keeping these liquids and re-using them. In effect, as they are re-used the flavors become more concentrated, which benefits the foods that are cooked in them.

Keep these points in mind, but feel free to experiment, adding your own personal touch. Bon appetit!

Preparation
At the outset, you must remember that in Chinese cooking the freshness of ingredients is of prime importance: the first step then is to assemble all the ingredients required for a recipe and to prepare them in one single operation just prior to cooking. Chinese cooking, even when done with a microwave oven requires that the ingredients retain their crispy texture and their nutritive value. It is for this reason that it makes more sense to do all your cutting and chopping before cooking—because food cooks so quickly in the microwave, those ingredients in the process of cooking may well overcook if you are busy preparing others for the same dish. As well, because the microwave permits such a quick and controlled method of cooking, you can afford to spend the time cutting up all the ingredients you will need beforehand.

All the ingredients that require the same treatment should be handled at the same time; for example, if carrots and celery are to be cut diagonally and peppers and bamboo shoots, in strips, do the one type of cutting and then the other. This methodical approach induces a sort of "rhythm" about your work, promoting efficiency and therefore saving time.

From Wok to Browning Dish

Since our section on microwave utensils and dishes on page 21 merely mentions the wok, essential to Chinese cooking, we shall now go into more detail about it. The word "wok" means "kitchen receptacle." In use for centuries in China, it has maintained its original form. It is a shallow pan with an open area under its base that conducts the heat while it sits in a raised position over the very hot flame used in traditional Chinese kitchens.

Since modern-day stoves (electric or gas) do not allow as much distance between the bottom of the wok and the heat source, a metal cylinder is placed between the wok and the heating element. This ring prevents the food from direct contact with too intense a heat source. The wok is especially recommended for sautéing food. Its concave form with shallow rounded sides makes it easy to stir-fry, lightly frying the food and then moving it up the sides out of the hot oil, which stays in the bottom of the pan.

But, as we all well know, metal cannot be used in the microwave oven and use of the wok is therefore out of the question. We do, however, have an effective substitute—the browning dish. Developed solely for use in the microwave oven, this dish has many advantages. It is square in shape but resembles the wok in other respects. The bottom of the dish is covered with ferrite, a substance that absorbs the microwaves and thus becomes very hot, browning any food place in it. The dish has four slightly raised legs so that it never comes in direct contact with the surface on which it rests. However, in spite of this design feature, never put a browning dish directly on your counter after cooking as the hot dish would damage it. And always use pot holders or oven mitts when handling the browning dish to avoid nasty burns. Used mainly to sear or brown fish, meat and vegetables that have been cut into small pieces, the browning dish can be used to brown larger cuts in order to give them a more pleasing color.

Easy to use, the browning dish permits the rapid cooking of food. Heat the dish for 7 minutes at 100% power, remove it, add a little vegetable oil and heat again at 100% for 30 seconds. Add the ingredients in steps, depending on the length of time each requires. The ferrite gives off such an intense heat that it will not be necessary, with some finely chopped items, to return the dish to the oven. Remember, you must stir the ingredients several times for even browning and cooking.

If you would like to take up traditional Chinese cooking as a hobby but feel your modern, hectic style of living won't permit it—take heart! Thanks to the microwave oven, the two styles are not incompatible.

Is It All Chinese to You?

Like all great arts, cooking, over the long years of its history, has developed its own specialized vocabulary to describe its techniques as well as different dishes. Since you will come across them quite frequently in this volume, we felt descriptions of some of the terms would be useful.

Aromatic: Plant, leaf or herb with a strong, distinctive aroma, used to add a pleasant, subtle taste to dishes.

Braise: To cook slowly in a small quantity of liquid over a gentle heat in a covered dish in order to keep all the juices in the meat.

Brown: To fry in oil or butter in order to give food a golden color.

Cleaver: A chinese knife with a wide, heavy blade used to chop meat, fish and vegetables.

Glaze: To brush the surface of meat with oil, butter, sauce or beaten eggs to give it a glossy appearance and to add flavor.

Marinate: To marinate for Chinese cooking is to soak meat in a mixture of soy sauce, garlic and such other flavoring agents as ginger and coriander in order to tenderize as well as to flavor it.

Poach: To simmer food very gently in liquid.

Reduce: To boil a mixture to evaporate surplus liquid to enhance the flavor and produce a thicker consistency.

Sake:	An alcoholic beverage of Japanese origin, made from fermented rice.
Sauté:	To cook vegetables or meat quickly by tossing in oil or butter on high heat.
Sear:	To give meat an initial browning over a very high heat.
Season:	To add salt, pepper or spices to food in order to enhance flavor.
Simmer:	To cook over gentle heat at just below the boiling point.
Slice:	To cut vegetables, fruit, meat or fish into very thin slices.
Strip:	A long, thin piece of meat or fish, cut lengthwise.
Tenderize:	To soften meats by marinating them, pounding them with a mallet or piercing them all over.
Truss:	To secure, by sewing or tying, the legs and wings of a bird so that it will not lose its shape during cooking.

Culinary Terms

Have you ever picked up a menu and found yourself at a loss to understand the names of the different dishes? Most of the terms used to describe oriental cooking are obscure in origin and, naturally, difficult for us to understand. We have therefore compiled a short glossary to help you with those difficult menus.

Ancient or thousand-year eggs: Duck eggs that have been preserved in a mixture of alkali, lime ashes, mud and other materials.

Bai chai: Dishes containing Chinese cabbage.

Cantonese cooking: The most well-known and most diversified style of Chinese cooking.

Chiang yu wong: Flavored with light soy sauce.

Hoisin: A paste or sweet sauce with a soy sauce base that is reddish in color.

Hzing zen: Flavored with almond essence.

Kiang: With ginger as a main flavoring agent.

Lo chou: With soy sauce as a main ingredient.

Mi-chiu: Flavored with sake.

Peking cooking: A style of cooking from the northern regions of China, specializing in sweet and sour dishes. Noodles or dumplings and lamb are frequently used in these dishes.

Shark fin: Long fillet cut close to the cartilage of the shark fin. The meat is very tender.

Swallow's nest: A gelatin-like substance extracted from the seaweed used by swallows to build their nests; usually served in a clear chicken broth.

Tong-kow: Winter melon soup.

Tsung: With sliced green onions as a garnish or an ingredient.

Yunnan ham: Smoked and salted, the characteristic flavor has made it a favorite with many gourmets.

Conversion Chart

Conversion Chart for the Main Measures Used in Cooking

Volume		Weight	
1 teaspoon	5 mL	2.2 lb	1 kg (1000 g)
1 tablespoon	15 mL	1.1 lb	500 g
		0.5 lb	225 g
1 quart (4 cups)	1 litre	0.25 lb	115 g
1 pint (2 cups)	500 mL		
1/2 cup	125 mL		
1/4 cup	50 mL	1 oz	30 g

Metric Equivalents for Cooking Temperatures

49°C	120°F	120°C	250°F
54°C	130°F	135°C	275°F
60°C	140°F	150°C	300°F
66°C	150°F	160°C	325°F
71°C	160°F	180°C	350°F
77°C	170°F	190°C	375°F
82°C	180°F	200°C	400°F
93°C	200°F	220°C	425°F
107°C	225°F	230°C	450°F

Readers will note that, in the recipes, we give 250 mL as the equivalent for 1 cup and 450 g as the equivalent for 1 lb and that fractions of these measurements are even less mathematically accurate. The reason for this is that mathematically accurate conversions are just not practical in cooking. Your kitchen scales are simply not accurate enough to weigh 454 g—the true equivalent of 1 lb—and it would be a waste of time to try. The conversions given in this series, therefore, necessarily represent approximate equivalents, but they will still give excellent results in the kitchen. No problems should be encountered if you adhere to either metric or imperial measurements throughout a recipe.

Index

MICROTIPS